quarterlife
CRISIS

quarterlife

CRI

Jeremy P. Tarcher / Putnam

a member of Penguin Putnam Inc.

New York

Alexandra Robbins

and Abby Wilner

The Unique Challenges of
Life in Your Twenties

Jeremy P. Tarcher/Putnam
a member of
Penguin Putnam Inc.
375 Hudson Street
New York, NY 10014
www.penguinputnam.com

Library of Congress Cataloging-in-Publication Data

Robbins, Alexandra, date.
    Quarterlife crisis : the unique challenges of life in your twenties / Alexandra Robbins and Abby Wilner.
      p.   cm.
    Includes index.
    ISBN 1-58542-106-5
    1. Adulthood—Psychological aspects.   2. Young adults—Conduct of life.   3. Young adults—Psychology.   I. Wilner, Abby, date.   II. Title.
    BF724.5 .R55   2001   00-066760
    158'.084'2—dc21

Acknowledgments

A number of people made writing this book a pleasure. Thanks, first and foremost, to my parents for their patience and support, to my siblings for keeping me company and entertaining me during long nights at the computer, and to my grandparents for their enthusiasm.

I am also eternally grateful to David Dashefsky for everything, Amy Lindenbaum for being the best a friend can be, Joe Klein for his encouragement, Andrea Kirk for her help with sources, Nick Bernstein for cracking me up, the Upstarts for humoring me, and Abby Wilner for inspiring me.

This book would not have been written but for Dick Victory, who urged me to do it; Jane Mayer, who kindly went out of her way to jump-start the process; and of course, Paula Balzer, who got it done patiently with a smile.

Finally, thanks to all of the twentysomethings who agreed to be interviewed for this book. You were honest, open, thoughtful, and articulate. You are the spokespersons for our generation.

—A.R.

Acknowledgments

Special thanks to:

"E&E"—for bringing me into this world and making my quarterlife crisis possible—and for raising me to believe I could accomplish anything, even publish a book.

Amy Dowis for the original idea to write a book for troubled twentysomethings, and the League for "inspiration," if you know what I mean.

Ellona, Tammy, and the friends who make me laugh, the runners who make me strong, and the neighbors of QHS11 who keep me company—thanks to all of you who turned my QLC into the most fabulous time.

The pros I know—Dr. Robert DuPont and Tony Pitch—who offered their expertise, believed in this book and encouraged me to make it happen.

Alex Robbins for dedicating yourself to the book and making my dream a reality.

Paula Balzer, of Sarah Lazin Books, and Jeremy P. Tarcher for taking a chance on us.

Finally, the hundred or so twentysomethings who made this book what it is by opening up and sharing their experiences. Thanks to you, people will realize just how common the quarterlife crisis really is. This huge transition—becoming an adult—has been completely overlooked, until now.

—A.W.

Contents

six: How Do I Work Out the Right Balance Among My Career, Friends, Family, and Romance?

seven: Can I Carry Any Part of My College Experience into the Real World?

conclusion

appendix

topical index

To Ira, Jo,

Andrew, Missy,

Rachel, Irving,

Seena and Marty,

with love

Preface

Our intention, when we first began to work on this book, was to get the idea of a quarterlife crisis into the national discourse. The more that people would use the term "quarterlife crisis," in any fashion, the more twentysomethings would hear it, relate to it, and know their own experiences were both common and legitimate. When members of the book industry warned us that it might be difficult to market a book to twentysomethings, we resigned ourselves to accepting the fact that the book might help a few scattered twentysomethings across the country who might see themselves in some of the stories. We never expected what followed.

Quarterlife Crisis: The Unique Challenges of Life in Your Twenties sparked an international dialogue, with widespread discussions on the radio, in newspapers, and on TV. Our book has been published in countries as diverse as England, Korea, and Brazil. We have heard from hundreds of twentysomethings across the world—including peers in Zimbabwe, Malaysia, and Singapore—most of whom have expressed variations on the same theme: "I thought I was alone."

We found this global phenomenon staggering: thousands, if not millions, of twentysomethings were experiencing similar identity issues, yet the vast majority of these young adults remained silent. Because the twenties are portrayed as—and therefore are "supposed" to be—such a carefree, rollicking good time, few people were willing to admit that they weren't actually having the time of their lives after all. Twentysomethings would get caught in a cycle:

1) They would be unhappy (or anxious or depressed).
2) They wouldn't talk about it.
3) Because they wouldn't discuss their problems, they wouldn't learn that these issues were common.
4) They thought something must be wrong with them individually.
5) Their self-doubt subsequently spiraled, and they became unhappier.

Luckily, this cycle is changing. It has become acceptable to talk about a "quarterlife crisis" with friends, at parties, in bars. New quarterlife crisis support groups are sprouting up around the nation specifically to allow twentysomethings to share their experiences with others, relate, and feel better. Young adults and recent graduates are learning now that the twentysomething years aren't supposed to be a constant high but rather a journey full of both successes and setbacks.

We, too, have journeyed far over the past year, from harboring humble expectations to discovering that our peers are eager and excited to assist and encourage one another. We thank you—readers, writers, and listeners—for accompanying us on this journey.

—The Authors
Spring 2002

quarterlife
CRISIS

introduction

What Is the Quarterlife Crisis?

J im, the neighbor who lives in the three-story colonial down the block, has recently turned 50. You know this because Jim's wife threw him a surprise party about a month ago. You also know this because, since then, Jim has dyed his hair blond, purchased a leather bomber jacket, traded in his Chevy Suburban for a sleek Miata, and ditched the wife for a girlfriend half her size and age.

Yet, aside from the local ladies' group's sympathetic clucks for the scorned wife, few neighbors are surprised at Jim's instant lifestyle change. Instead, they nod their heads understandingly. "Oh, Jim," they say. "He's just going through a midlife crisis. Everyone goes through it." Friends, colleagues, and family members excuse his weird behavior as an inevitable effect of reaching this particular stage of life. Like millions of other middle-aged people, Jim has reached a period during which he believes he must ponder the direction of his life—and then alter it.

Chances are, if you're reading this book, you're not Jim. You know this because you can't afford a leather bomber jacket, you drive your parents' Volvo (if you drive a car at all), and, regardless of your gender, you would happily marry Jim's wife if she gets to keep the house. But Jim's midlife crisis is relevant to you nonetheless, because it is currently the only age-related crisis that is widely recognized as a common, inevitable part of life. This is pertinent because, despite all of the attention lavished on the midlife crisis, despite the hundreds of books, movies, and magazine articles dedicated to explaining the sometimes traumatic transition through middle age and the ways to cope with it, the midlife crisis is not the only age-related crisis that we experience. As Yoda whispered to Luke Skywalker, "There is another."

This other crisis can be just as, if not more, devastating than the midlife crisis. It can throw someone's life into chaotic disarray or paralyze it completely. It may be the single most concentrated period during which individuals relentlessly question their future and how it will follow the events of their past. It covers the interval that encompasses the transition from the academic world to the "real" world—an age group that can range from late adolescence to the mid-thirties but is usually most intense in twentysomethings. It is what we call the quarterlife crisis, and it is a real phenomenon.

The quarterlife crisis and the midlife crisis stem from the same basic problem, but the resulting panic couldn't be more opposite. At their cores, both the quarterlife crisis and the midlife crisis are about a major life change. Often, for people experiencing a midlife crisis, a sense of stagnancy sparks the need for change. During this period, a middle-aged person tends to reflect on his past, in part to see if his life to date measures up to the life he had envisioned as a child (or as a twenty-something). The midlife crisis also impels a middle-aged person to look forward, sometimes with an increasing sense of desperation, at the time he feels he has left.

In contrast, the quarterlife crisis occurs precisely because there is none of that predictable stability that drives middle-aged people to do unpredictable things. After about twenty years in a sheltered school setting—or more if a person has gone on to graduate or professional school—many graduates undergo some sort of culture shock. In the academic environment, goals were clear-cut and the ways to achieve them were mapped out distinctly. To get into a good college or graduate school, it helped if you graduated with honors; to graduate with honors, you needed to get good grades; to get good grades, you had to study hard. If your goals were athletic, you worked your way up from junior varsity or walk-on to varsity by practicing skills, working out in the weight room, and gelling with teammates and coaches. The better you were, the more playing time you got, the more impressive your statistics could become.

But after graduation, the pathways blur. In that crazy, wild nexus that people like to call the "real world," there is no definitive way to get from point A to point B, regardless of whether the points are related to a career, financial situation, home, or social life (though we have found through several unscientific studies that offering to pay for the next round of drinks can usually improve three out of the four). The extreme uncertainty that twentysomethings experience after graduation occurs because what was once a solid line that they could follow throughout their series of educational institutions has now disintegrated into millions of different options. The sheer number of possibilities can certainly inspire hope—that is why people say that twentysomethings have their whole lives ahead of them. But the endless array of decisions can also make a recent graduate feel utterly lost.

So while the midlife crisis revolves around a doomed sense of stagnancy, of a life set on pause while the rest of the world rattles on, the quarterlife crisis is a response to overwhelming instability, constant change, too many choices, and a panicked sense of helplessness. Just as the monotony of a lifestyle stuck in idle can drive a person to question himself intently, so, too, can the uncertainty of a life thrust into chaos. The transition from childhood to adulthood—from school to the world beyond—comes as a jolt for which many of today's twentysomethings simply are not prepared. The resulting overwhelming senses of helplessness and cluelessness, of indecision and apprehension, make up the real and common experience we call the quarterlife crisis. Individuals who are approaching middle age at least know what is coming. Because the midlife crisis is so widely acknowledged, people who undergo it are at the very least aware that there are places where they can go for help, such as support groups, books, movies, or Internet sites. Twentysomethings, by contrast, face a crisis that hits them with a far more powerful force than they ever expected. The slam is particularly painful because today's twentysomethings believe that they are alone and that they are having a much more difficult transition period than their peers—because the twenties are supposed to be "easy," because no one talks about these problems, and because the difficulties are therefore so unexpected. And at the fragile, doubt-ridden age during which the quarterlife crisis occurs, the ramifications can be extremely dangerous.

Why Worry About a Quarterlife Crisis?

The whirlwind of new responsibilities, new liberties, and new choices can be entirely overwhelming for someone who has just emerged from the shelter of twenty years of schooling. We don't mean to make graduates sound as if they have been hibernating since they emerged from the womb; certainly it is not as if they have been slumbering throughout adolescence (though some probably tried). They have in a sense, however, been encased in a bit of a cocoon, where someone or something—parents or school, for example—has protected them from a lot of the scariness of their surroundings. As a result, when graduates are let loose into the world, their dreams and desires can be tinged with trepidation. They are hopeful, but at the same time they are also, to put it simply, scared silly.

Some might say that because people have had to deal with the rite of passage from youth to adulthood since the beginning of time, this crisis is not really a "crisis" at all, given that historically this transitional period has, at various times, been marked with ceremonial rituals involving things like spears and buffalo dung. Indeed, it may not always have been a crisis.

But it has become one.

Maybe it is because the career and financial opportunities for college graduates have skyrocketed in the past decade and, therefore, so has the pressure to succeed. Maybe it is because the crazy people out there who amuse themselves by going on shooting rampages seem to have proliferated in recent years, leaving young adults more fearful of entering into relationships with new friends, lovers, and roommates. Or maybe increasing competition from the rising millions of fellow students has left twentysomethings feeling like they have to work harder than ever to stand out from their peers. Whatever the reason, the quarterlife crisis poses enough of a threat to the well-being of many graduates—however well-adjusted they may be—that it has to be taken seriously. Here's why.

Although hope is a common emotion for twentysomethings, hopelessness has become just as widespread. The revelation that life simply isn't easy—a given for some twentysomethings, a mild inconvenience for others, but a shattering blow for several—is one of the most distressing aspects of the quarterlife crisis, particularly for individuals who do not have large support networks or who doubt themselves often. It is in these situations that the quarterlife crisis becomes not just a common stage—it can become hazardous. Not everyone at the age of the quarterlife encounters some sort of depression, which is why we relegate doubts and depression to only one chapter. But we are addressing depression as one common result of the quarterlife crisis here so that we can illustrate why it is so important to acknowledge this transition period.

After interviewing dozens of twentysomethings who said they were depressed because of the transition, we ran our conclusions by Robert DuPont, a Georgetown Medical School professor of psychology who wrote *The Anxiety Cure*. "Based on my experience," DuPont said, "I have found that there is a high rate of all forms of disorder in this age group, including addiction, anxiety, depression, and many other kinds of problems because of the high stress associated with the transition from being a child to being an adult. And that has gotten more stressful as the road map has become less used. The old way of doing this was to get out and get it done right away. There was an economic imperative to doing it. It's not like that anymore. And as the road map has disappeared, the stress has gone up. People have to invent their own road map. It used to be that it came with the college graduation. Now you have to go out and figure it out yourself."

These high rates of disorders, however, have gone virtually unacknowledged. That's why we can't bog you down with statistics on this age group. They don't exist. Psychological research on twentysomethings, including statistics on depression and suicide, has not been performed. We asked major national mental health associations such as the National Institutes of Mental Health, the American Psychiatric Association, and the National Depressive and Manic Depressive Association for any information they had on people in their twenties. They didn't have any. As one psychologist told us, associations don't cut the data to incorporate this age group. "It's not a subject that's interesting to them. They just lump everybody together," he said.

We can only speculate as to why there are no psychological studies on our age group:

❖ The public and the media largely ignore 21- to 35-year-olds as a generation.

❖ Because many twentysomethings cannot afford therapy, professionals do not have accurate and representative records of graduates' depression.

❖ Twentysomethings tend to attach a stigma to therapy—so they do not talk about it.

So we can't tell you the percentage of people who experience depression at some point during their twentysomething years. We can't tell you the likelihood that the transition from college to the real world will create such a jolt that a twentysomething will experience something more than the normal anxiety. And we can't tell you how many twentysomethings see therapists. All we can do in this book is provide you with our interview-based conclusions (lots, high, and many more than you think) and the stories of more than one hundred of the twentysomethings with whom we spoke.

How Do You Recognize a Quarterlife Crisis?

While at its heart the quarterlife crisis is an identity crisis, it causes twentysomethings' conflicting emotions to show up in different ways. Sometimes they reach a state of panic sparked by a feeling of loss and uncertainty. When the carefree euphoria that accompanies graduation wanes, many twentysomethings realize that things seem to be missing from their lives. The friends who were just around the corner in college have scattered, the social life that had been as easy as meeting someone in the bathroom down the hall has dissipated, and the mandatory assignments that provided structure and purpose have (however thankfully) been completed. Whether they immediately begin a frantic online job search or collapse into a vegetative state in front of Comedy Central, it eventually sets in that things have changed. The world is suddenly unfamiliar as graduates come to realize that four or more years of higher education have hardly prepared them for the decisions they will have to make and the ways in which they will have to learn to support themselves. Twentysomethings often feel that the only means they have for navigating the seemingly endless choices looming ahead of them is trial and error, which is really just a productive-sounding euphemism for guesswork. Welcome to the casino: the confusion and helplessness that strike millions of twentysomethings soon after graduation is frequently the result of the feeling that they are about to gamble. Often. On their lives.

For some people the quarterlife crisis is both a cause and an effect of procrastination and denial. Building on the image of that guy who is vegging in front of the television, a big part of twentysomethings' attempts to adjust to their new lives involves stalling like they have never stalled before. Granted, many ambitious students line up jobs while they are still in school. But by the same token, many do not. And even the ones who do still find their transition is far from seamless. Some of this difficulty may have to do with the fact that the once-reliable support network of parents and relatives is not quite sufficient anymore. The economic landscape, which is even now constantly changing for twentysomethings, differs greatly from the landscape of their parents' generation. Dot coms did not exist. The technology sector was piddling compared to what it is now. Aspiring doctors went to medical school, lawyers went to law school, and teachers attained degrees in education. Job and life patterns were more clear-cut, and there was less emphasis on "love what you do" in favor of "support the family." People married and had children at a much younger age. Things were different. What this means for today's graduates is that, because job opportunities have changed so drastically in the past generation, they must place much more accountability on themselves. Frequently that is something they are not yet ready to accept.

Another way the quarterlife crisis can show up, particularly in the mid- to late twenties, is in a feeling of disappointment, of "This is all there is?" Maybe the job turns out to be not so glamorous after all, or maybe it just doesn't seem to lead anywhere interesting. Perhaps the year of travel in Europe was more of a wallet buster than previously imagined—even with nights in youth hostels and meals of ramen. Or maybe the move to a hip, new city just didn't turn out to be as fabulous a relocation as expected.

While these are, according to older generations, supposed to be the best years of their lives, twentysomethings also feel that the choices they make during this period will influence their thirties, forties, fifties, and on, in an irreparable domino effect. As a result, twentysomethings frequently have the unshakable belief that this is the time during which they have to nail down the meaning in their lives, which explains why they often experience a nagging feeling that somehow they need to make their lives more fulfilling. This is why there are so many drastic life changes at this point in life: an investment banker breaks off his engagement and volunteers for the Peace Corps; a consultant suddenly frets that consulting may not really have that much influence on other people's lives; a waiter chucks the steady paycheck to live in his car and try to make it in Hollywood; a law school graduate decides she doesn't want to be a lawyer after all and seeks a job in technology.

The changes hurtling toward a young adult, as well as the potential for more changes ahead, can be excruciatingly overwhelming for someone who is trying so hard to figure out how to feel fulfilled. A lot of people don't realize just how suffocating this pressure can be. The prevalent belief is that twentysomethings have it relatively easy because they do not have as many responsibilities as older individuals. But it is precisely this reduced responsibility that renders the vast array of decisions more difficult to make. For instance, if there were, say, a family to consider, a mother might not be as inclined to take a risk on the stock market. If a guy's elderly father were sick, he probably wouldn't take that year off to travel in South America. Twentysomethings, for the most part, just aren't at those stages yet, which is why they are sometimes envied. But because their choices aren't narrowed down for them by responsibilities, they have more decisions to make. And while this isn't necessarily bad, it can make things pretty complex. Figuring out which changes to make in order to make life more fulfilling is hard enough. But deciding to make a change and then following through with it requires an extraordinary amount of strength, which is sometimes hard to come by for a recent graduate who has not had to rely solely on himself for very long.

The most widespread, frightening, and quite possibly the most difficult manifestation of the quarterlife crisis is a feeling that can creep up on a twentysomething whether he is unemployed, living at home, and friendless, or in an interesting job, with a great apartment, and dozens of buddies. Regardless of their levels of self-esteem, confidence, and overall well-being, twentysomethings are particularly vulnerable to doubts. They doubt their decisions, their abilities, their readiness, their past, present, and future . . . but most of all, they doubt themselves. The twenties comprise a period of intense questioning—of introspection and self-development that young adults often feel they are not ready for. The questions can range from seemingly trivial choices—"Should I really have spent $100 to join that fantasy baseball league?"—to irrefutably mammoth decisions—"When is the right time for me to start a family?" It is healthy, of course, for people to question themselves some; an occasional self-assessment or life inventory is a natural part of the quest for improvement. But if the questioning becomes constant and the barrage of doubts never seems to cease, twentysomethings can feel as if it is hard to catch their breath, as if they are spiraling downward. Many times the doubts increase because twentysomethings think it is abnormal to have them in the first place. No one talks about having doubts at this age, so when twentysomethings do find that they are continuously questioning themselves, they think something is wrong with them.

What Do You Do About the Quarterlife Crisis?

Hopefully, this book will help to change that perception. This book won't solve the quarterlife crisis, just as the hundreds of books on the midlife crisis won't make anybody any younger. But the first way to confront the quarterlife crisis is to acknowledge that there is one. We came up with some of the deepest questions that are plaguing twenty-somethings—the questions that they ask themselves but do not ask each other and the types of inquiries that might have come up during one of those three A.M. philosophical discussions that were so common in college and so rare after graduation. Then we asked these questions to twentysomethings across the country. In this book, they share their uncertainties, their indecisiveness, and their failures—as well as their successes and how they achieved them. When other twentysomethings realize that the barrage of doubts they face on a regular basis is not that uncommon, maybe these limbo years will seem a bit less daunting.

The lack of psychological studies on relatively recent college gradu-ates ties in to a larger problem for individuals in this age group: twenty-somethings are virtually invisible in the marketplace. Perhaps one of the most noticeable differences between the midlife crisis and the quarterlife crisis is that, until now, no one had bothered to name and to address the twentysomething years as an often traumatic and wholly unrecognized difficult turning point in life. This lack of acknowledg-ment, of course, has simply fueled the quarterlife crisis into an even more difficult experience. Because graduates are not made aware that other graduates are experiencing the same cyclone of doubts, they doubt themselves to an even greater extent. Considering the fact that nearly every possible mental ailment, confusion, or inconvenience has a name now, from the well-established postpartum depression and attention deficit/hyperactivity disorder to the lesser-known medical students' disorder and inanimate object phobia, we found it surprising that no one had yet come up with a name for the tough shift from student life to real life.

Our critics, once they surface, might counter that no one had named the quarterlife crisis because such a crisis does not exist. The reason we wrote this book is precisely because of that mind-set. Nearly all of the twentysomethings we spoke to believed that their identity crises were unusual, which only made them feel more isolated. But the funny thing was that all of them were going through pretty much the same experience.

One reason today's twentysomethings may feel so alone could be that it is so difficult to lump them together as a group. They do not have a strong, collectively shared historical moment that helped to define them and continues to shape their identity. The baby boomers had the Vietnam War and its aftermath, the Kennedy assassinations, Martin Luther King, Jr.'s speeches, and the civil rights movement. Americans older than the baby boomers had the Great Depression, the World Wars, and the Cold War. Today's children and teenagers are the first generation to grow up in the Information Age, with computers as a necessity and the Internet as a primary method of communication. They also share the horror that schools simply are not safe anymore. What do twentysomethings have? They have the Challenger explosion, which was unquestionably a tragic event, but it did not leave a legacy that caused them to debate issues or shift principles. It was just sad. They have the Persian Gulf War, which seemed too distant, too minor to those who weren't fighting in it or who didn't personally know someone stationed in the Middle East. There were no protests or parades akin to the attention America devoted to the other major wars of the century. The death of Kurt Cobain may be the closest thing twentysomethings have to an event that gave them a collective sense of tragedy, of shared grief, of a historical mark that influenced all of their lives as a generation. But it didn't, really. It hurt, and it frustrated, and it angered, but it didn't draw twentysomethings together as one common unit. Nothing really has.

By now you will probably have noticed that we refer to the people who are prime targets for the quarterlife crisis as twentysomethings. We do this for two reasons. First of all, "quarterlifers" somehow just doesn't sound right—we don't call 40-to-60-year-olds "midlifers," and we certainly don't call centenarians "endlifers." Dude, that would just be mean. Second, the term that the public and the media most often use to describe this age range is "GenXers." People completely gloss over the fact that twentysomethings simply do not have the sense of collectivity that the boomers and the horrifically named younger "GenYers" supposedly share. Generation X was the name of Billy Idol's band and the title of a 1965 British self-help manual. For some reason, in 1991, Douglas Coupland used the term to describe twentysomethings in his book *Generation X: Tales for an Accelerated Culture*. Marketers pounced on the term, and suddenly the members of this thirteenth generation since the Pilgrims landed found the label Generation X affixed permanently to their backs. It stuck. But the phrase Generation X means absolutely nothing to the generation it is supposed to encompass. We are not going to refer to ourselves and our peers with a label that we do not understand. In our opinion, there are really only two things that apply to most twentysomethings: they are, obviously, the same age; and they tend to fall into crisis mode at this point in their lives.

We realize that this book at times may come across like a program on the Nature Channel: "Here we observe the twentysomething in its natural habitat. See it feed on Pop-Tarts and caffeine. Watch as it struggles to decide whether to return to its birthplace or strike out on its own." But for other generations, twentysomethings can be a bit of a mystery. That is why, while we are primarily gearing this book for twentysomethings, we are also writing it for the people who want to get a better grasp of what it is like to be a twentysomething today.

The twentysomethings in this book are a diverse crowd, from dozens of universities and dozens of geographical areas across the country. They are people who earned their undergraduate degrees some time during the past ten years. They come from a variety of ethnic, economic, moral, racial, and religious backgrounds. We intend this book to represent their voices, not as one collective expression, but rather as a collage of different voices that speak separately, yet largely come together. Currently, the twentysomething generation has no spokesperson, no one who represents the interests of recent graduates as a group. We are hoping that the twentysomethings in this book will emerge as a group of voices that can in some fashion, however vague, speak for all of us.

You might be reading this book because you yourself are a twentysomething who is in the midst of or has already experienced the quarterlife crisis. Or you might be a college or graduate student who is curious about this sometimes shattering shift and wants to prepare for the transition to come. Or maybe you are a concerned parent, friend, colleague, teacher, neighbor, or relative who merely wants to understand what it is like to be a twentysomething in the twenty-first century and how to help the twentysomethings you know ease into adulthood as smoothly as possible. Then again, perhaps you are the middle-aged Jim after all, complete with leather jacket and Miata, in which case you should probably pay particularly close attention so that you can better understand the mood swings of your brand new girlfriend.

one
How Am I Supposed to Figure Out Who I Really Am?

The quest to define ourselves begins during childhood, but when twentysomethings enter the "real" world, the process can seem to start all over again. This experience is difficult partly because a person has to go through it alone, and during a time when many aspects of life are already in pandemonium. It is under these circumstances that the quarterlife crisis is truly an identity crisis. When recent graduates are tossed from a school setting, they have to figure out everything in the real world quickly; but at the same time, and more important, they have to remember to figure themselves out, too. The twentysomethings with whom we spoke told us that they have coped or are coping with this transition using a combination of the right attitude, determination, openmindedness, and, often, a whole lot of luck.

Jeff,* a 24-year-old resident of Wilmington, Delaware, says that, for twentysomethings, figuring themselves out is a daily process that can occasionally consist of surprising revelations. "Every day there's a

---

*Throughout, some names and identifying details have been changed.

different situation that can teach you something new about yourself," Jeff says. "I've wanted a dog for the past ten years, ever since mine died. In that time I've been able to construct a pretty good image of what I want in a dog. My dog should be big and brawny (I'm a big guy) and tough and all of the things you would expect in a 'man's dog.' I thought I would be able to train it from puppyhood so it would be the best dog I could make it. So my girlfriend and I went to the animal shelter to pick out a puppy. We looked them over, but most were already taken. They told us that later on in the week, they would have some Siberian husky–German shepherd mixes available. Those are fairly big dogs, so I thought, 'Great!'

"Well, on our way out," Jeff says, "I just happened to look to my left and this dog stood up and looked at me with a really funny look. So of course, I stopped and looked it over. It seemed a little shy and was listed as a quiet, friendly four-year-old *little* dog. Needless to say, today we are very happy with our little beagle. I never thought I would own a 'little' dog." Jeff uses this experience to continuously remind himself that things don't always happen as planned. "Since almost every situation is a little different from the last, we are always being challenged on how we will react to the variations. So even if you've wanted to be a doctor all your life (like my sister), you may still end up in a management training program for a big supply company. The day that everything in your life is settled and you've learned everything about you there is to learn is the day that your body has decided to call it quits and your mind doesn't think that's such a bad idea."

"So, What Do You Do?"

Many twentysomethings find that the easiest way to attempt to pinpoint their identity after graduation is to define who they are by what they do. When they have a job description, they sometimes try to apply it to their identities, because that's often the only constant they have. The reasoning is hardly far-fetched—several twentysomethings point out that within the first few minutes of a conversation with someone they have just met, one person will ask what the other person does for a living. When the person responds, the inquirer subconsciously passes judgement. But because so many recent graduates are dissatisfied with their first couple of jobs after college, the idea that their jobs make up a large part of who they are can leave them feeling dejected.

"Notions of 'self' were thrown around all of the time during my time at college," says Gabriella, a 1996 graduate of Oberlin College (Ohio). "Going to a *liberal* liberal arts school, we all practically majored in being incredibly self-aware, probably bordering on neurotic and self-indulgent—sometimes luxurious, sometimes delusional, mostly a mixture of both. But it was always somehow a safe topic to discuss from the distance of academic jargon, literary and pop culture references, and silly gossip. When I graduated and wasn't defined anymore by what I was studying and where I went to school, I was really struck by how much I *didn't* have my 'self' figured out. Without the easy structure of school that I'd been used to all of my life, I noticed how everything else was pretty fluid or changeable in my life. Was I changing? Was everyone else? What to do?"

Gabriella says that twentysomethings believe they have to define themselves by their jobs because they have just emerged from school, where their identities were generally aligned with their studies and their activities. "I think many people, especially in American middle- and upper-class culture, go directly from college to defining themselves by their jobs. This makes me quite uneasy," she says. "I couldn't really say that the job I have right now—jewelry design and sales—really describes me as a person, even though I like it a lot. It's not my life's work. It's a strange and unnatural pressure that we feel upon graduation to hurry up, 'grow up,' and enter the 'real world' (a phrase I think represents an MTV show or a myth rather than a real thing), to devote the rest of your life to work and the next paycheck. This isn't me. No one should find herself in a job description."

Gabriella confronted the twentysomething trend of defining one's self by one's job by rebelling against it, an act that in itself helped her learn more about herself than she otherwise might have. By retreating from the mainstream rather than throwing herself head-on into it, Gabriella was able to find a better perspective for herself. "I left college not knowing what I wanted to do, and I still don't, but I'm finding out a lot about myself, and I'm more content because of my adventures and not some high salary. I figured out pretty quickly that I *didn't* want to be defined by my job, I didn't want to become part of corporate America, and that I'd figure out some way to live and be content. So I started traveling and I've learned so much about other cultures and other people, and in turn, about my own beliefs, strengths, and weaknesses. It's an especially trying time in life now, though, as everyone is going through the same questions, re-evaluations, and worries. There seems to be no balance or center at times. I think it would have been more difficult for me to work out grand questions of what makes me happy, what my values are, and what I want to do with my future if I had buckled down and gotten a serious office job, as that would have led me into a rut of regular routine. It helps that most of us in this age group are going through the same things. We could form a community based around this sort of crisis of self that we're all facing. I think this helps us all out more than everything else— the open dialogues at parties and bars and offices and reunions. We are all constantly changing, even in small ways, but this major transition jolts us all into some sort of nervous readjustment. All of a sudden we feel like we need concrete answers to everything, but that's pretty unrealistic."

The twentysomething experience, in Gabriella's words, is a time at which a "crisis of self" occurs. What can complicate this crisis even further is that twentysomethings generally do not talk about it; the opportunities to share profound, introspective insights about their identities just don't come up too often after college. As a result, many recent graduates do not realize that so many other people are going through the same questioning process.

Lindsey, a 26-year-old who lives in San Francisco, says the title of this chapter particularly resonated with her because it seems like everyone but her knows exactly what they are doing. "While I feel like I have known for a while who I am, I do not know how to translate this into a job or career. Traveling abroad has made me realize that here in the United States, when someone asks a stranger 'What do you do?', 'do' usually refers to a job and doesn't have anything to do with whether the person dances, is an activist on the side, has a family, takes classes, paints, and so on. So the question of what I will 'do' with my life has been plaguing me since graduation. I have always known things I like to do (such as working directly with people, often kids, often from another country or background), but never has one career, or even a job, jumped out at me as being the obvious vessel for my passions. I have never felt I fit into any typical career mold. Career services at my school didn't help me either—it was very difficult to find anything that wasn't corporate or graduate school. I used to always think (and for the most part I still do) that one day it would all suddenly gel—that what I am passionate about and love to do would turn out to be my job . . . or that I would come across a job where I would instantly know *that* is for me. After two years and the fact that I am moving on to my third job (I don't know what yet), I am beginning to get restless and at times frustrated. I often ask myself (even though part of me knows it is not true): how come everyone else around me knows what they want to *do*?"

What Now?

But even if it seems like everyone knows what they want to do at this point in their lives, there's no guarantee that what they want to do now will be what they always want to do. "Just over four years out of college,

I find that I am unsure about whether I am following the career path that is right for me," says Scott, a 1996 graduate of Oklahoma State University (Stillwater). "It's strange, because my professional situation now couldn't be more perfect—at least as I envisioned it when I graduated from school. In fact, I have achieved exactly what I set out to do, and it didn't come easy. Unlike my friends, I opted not to take a high-paying job in corporate finance or management consulting and instead chose to pursue the career I knew in my heart I was passionate about: politics. But politics is not an easy field to get into, and I had to start from the bottom—the very bottom. While my friends were earning forty thousand–plus a year in their first jobs, living on their own and experiencing the postcollegiate single life, I was working for free as a campaign volunteer and waiting tables at night to make a little spending money that I could use to have fun while I was living at home with my parents. But I knew hard work would pay off in the end, and I climbed the ladder fast. Finally, two and a half years later, I had the Capitol Hill job I'd dreamed of and worked toward, and it felt good. I still love my job, my office, my friends at work, even my boss. But it's not fulfilling."

For Scott, a successful search for a dream job in his early twenties has merely been replaced by a hunt for his "life's work" in his late twenties. "Who knew four years ago I'd actually want to be fulfilled by my work? But I do, and now I find myself questioning how and when I will find my life's work. I am, after all, nearly 27 years old. Some of my friends are getting married, for Christ's sake. One even has a kid. And here I am stranded in a never-never land of my own making. I've committed myself to exploring other options that interest me, but I'm having a hard time actually thinking of a career that sounds appealing. There is one that I've been meaning to explore, but sometimes I'd rather just watch TV or play guitar or go out with my friends. So maybe I'm not really meant to do that, either. When is something going to fall from the sky and hit me on the head, knock me out, and when I wake up I see clearly the road that lies ahead? Am I behind the curve? When will I know? That's the question."

Even when twentysomethings know exactly what they want to do for a living—and have somehow already managed to attain that job—it doesn't mean they have figured out everything they want to know about themselves. Helen, a 1996 graduate of the University of Texas at Austin, is a successful businesswoman who is in a job she enjoys because she achieved the position she had gunned for. "I always knew I wanted to be in business," she says. "So I looked for a college with a good business school, got a scholarship, and later graduated with two business degrees. After graduation I was hired into a corporate training program at a marketing company and I was on my way. The only question was, on my way to what? You see, all that time everything was in a sense already outlined for me. Go to school, get good grades, graduate, and get a good job. Now it was all done. I followed the outline to the letter like I was 'supposed to.' The next step, I figured, was to get promoted to manager. So three promotions later, I became a manager."

Now that Helen had gotten what she had wished for, however, everything else in her life didn't automatically settle into place as she had hoped. And now that she had suddenly reached the pinnacle of the career path she had envisioned for herself, she didn't know what to do next. "For the first time in my life, I felt like there was no new topic in my outline," she says. "I got what I had zeroed in on. And now I was wondering, what do I do next? There has to be a 'next.' There has always been a 'next' in my life. After high school there was 'go to college,' after college there was 'get a job,' and then in your job it was 'work hard and get promoted.' So there I was, a twentysomething single, successful marketing manager, wondering what in the world the next step should be for me. I still haven't figured it out. But what I did learn is that all that time I spent wondering why I didn't have a plan and trying to figure out how to get one, my *real* life was passing me by. Do I look at others my age and make life comparisons? Of course. I'm human. But no one has the 'right answer.' There is no *best* plan to follow. I think that is the scariest thing. You can't study and then pass the test. You can't work hard and get promoted. At the end of the day, I decide if my life is how I want it to be. Welcome to the real world. It's not exactly what I'd thought it'd be, but here I am."

Compromising Positions

One thing some twentysomethings have learned in their quest to figure out what they really want and then how to get it is that it often helps to be willing to compromise at least a little bit. Whether they convince themselves to lower their standards, shift their focus, or simply change their perspective, some twentysomethings say that what seemed to be a sacrifice in the short term actually made them better off in the long run. For Devon, a 27-year-old living in Houston, this seeming sacrifice involved her geographic location.

"See, I lucked out here," she says. "I've known that I wanted to be an art teacher since I was at least six years old. I know this for sure because about three years ago, I found a little essay I wrote in first grade about what I wanted to be when I grew up. In college, I was not the most scholarly of students, and I was definitely a little 'out there,' but the one thing I *did* know was that wherever I ended up teaching, it would be far away from Houston. I couldn't wait to get away from that place."

So when Devon applied for jobs after graduation, she looked everywhere but home. "I actually almost had my 'dream job'—it was a full-time elementary-school teaching job. Exactly what I wanted. When I interviewed, I was poised and confident. I schmoozed the principal, I oohed and aahed a board of twelve people and never let them see me sweat. The principal told me I was one of his top-choice candidates

and we began discussing salary. Then I got in a car accident. Everything changed. I went back to my fourth interview at my 'dream'
school to meet again with my 'dream' boss. He told me that I needed
to be back for my final interview the next morning. I told him that I
was unable to do that because I had been in a car accident and had
made prior arrangements to fly home that night because I didn't have a
car and I didn't have the money to just cancel the flight. I even took out
the picture of my car that had made the newspaper and handed it to
him so that he knew I wasn't making this up. He told me that if I truly
wanted the job I would be there. I told him that I truly wanted the
job and was prepared to sign a contract on the spot. He told me no.
'This is the real world now, Devon. You're not in college anymore,' he
said. 'If you want the job, you'll find a way to be here. Goodbye.' I
was crushed."

Although it hadn't even remotely been on her original radar screen,
another job possibility presented Devon with a Plan B. "It took me a
while to realize that I probably didn't want to work for that bastard anyway," she says. "As luck would have it, when my hometown school district found out that I had been in an accident, they held the job interview
open for me for an extra week. I interviewed at my home district, what
I assumed to be a courtesy interview for amusement purposes, really.
(I used to have multicolored hair and wear fishnets.) I showed up with a
suit, glasses, and a portfolio, and was in full character to fit the costume.
They seemed impressed, or perhaps amused, I thought. I went through
the whole interviewing process and was invited to teach a class. I figured
I was so young, with no experience, so they would never hire me—they
were just getting a kick out of me. Okay, I thought, they want a show,
damn it, I'll give them a *good* one. I showed up in front of a classroom of
random high school kids not much younger than me and in front of two
principals and an art teacher. I didn't even break a sweat. I even had a
good time. I can't tell you how surprised I was when they offered me the

job. I'm convinced the only reason I got this job was because I didn't think I had a shot in hell. I am now not only teaching in Houston, but at the very school that I graduated from just nine years ago, which isn't nearly as drabby as I had decided in my teenage angst not all that long ago."

Devon compromised her location for her career. By contrast, Penny, who graduated in 1999 from Syracuse University (New York) with a marketing degree, compromised her entire outlook. Penny was one of those people who thought she had everything figured out in time for adulthood. So she was unprepared for the dizzying questioning period of the quarterlife crisis. "I left college with the steadfast and newfound expectations of a child, and welcomed change with open arms. Everyone always thought I would be fine moving on, and the last person who would possibly move back home. But by some strange twist of events, and to my dismay, both proved to be false," she says. "I was delving into the most introspective time ever. I knew what I was passionate about (alternative medicine) but didn't have a degree in it. I knew where I wanted to live (out west) but didn't go there. I knew (or so I thought) what I wanted in a man, so I stayed with him and then questioned some more. It turned into a surreal cycle, and I started to retreat into my head and disconnect from the mind-body experience. For the past year I have been almost watching things pan out, as if a narrator to my own life."

First, Penny was flown to Ohio to interview twice for a position that she thought would be good for her career. Sure that she had the job, she began to plan for a new life in nearly deserted cornfields on the outskirts of Columbus. Weeks later, she found out she hadn't gotten the job after all. "When the smoke cleared, there I was in 'temporary' living conditions back at home and no one out of state wanted to interview me because of the risk of my not moving," she says. "Suddenly I *wasn't* moving on so well and started getting nostalgic. My boyfriend was still in school in Syracuse, and I sure as hell didn't want to continue the long-distance thing."

Penny then experienced a series of events that would eventually force her to reexamine the life she had previously been so sure she would lead. She ended up getting a job that she quit the day before she was supposed to start because she received an offer in the marketing department of a company in the natural health industry. She couldn't wake up in the morning and get excited about penetrating a market niche, but she went to work anyway. To be brief, this is how her first year out of college unfolded. She joined a gym, met people, learned that she was not assertive enough in an office environment while over-assertive in a social environment, picked up office politics, shunned office politics, learned that the initiative she had displayed in college wasn't worth anything in entry level employment, and traveled back and forth to Syracuse to visit her boyfriend. When her boyfriend got into a life-threatening accident and she risked her job to visit him in the hospital, he told her, "You didn't have to come." She realized she needed to make a change, the year 2000 came, and she didn't change anything (while at the same time, as she says, "everything was changing" around her). Eventually, she broke up with her boyfriend, bought a new car, and then crashed it.

Now she has quit her job. She dates, enjoys the sunshine, does more yoga, and is currently in the midst of doing what she calls "reconnecting." Upon reflection, Penny says she was focusing so hard on fitting into her perceived image of herself that she lost sight of who she actually was. "For the past year, all I worried about was who I really was, instead of 'just being,' like Pooh," she says. "Only in the past few weeks have I sat down and realized just how young I am and forgotten about my universal purpose for more than five minutes. It's extremely freeing and I need more of it. I've figured out what I want to do with my life, but that could change tomorrow. It all depends on whom I listen to on each shoulder. I don't feel that anyone is completely settled—it's all only a state of mind. We are ever-changing beings gravitating towards homeostasis. It seems we will truly learn about who we are and our life's path only after we have already taken the road less traveled—our own unique existence."

Like Penny, Samantha, a 25-year-old living in Minneapolis, attempted to ignore her instincts in order to follow the path she thought would be more practical, proper, and impressive to pursue. She had always considered teaching as a possible career because of her love for children. "But in college," she says, "I started to doubt that it was the right career choice for me. The low pay and low prestige made me feel like I should find another path—something that would sound impressive at my high school reunion. I majored in psychology as an undergraduate, thinking that I would eventually find something that 'clicked'—a job that I would love, that would pay well, and that would make my parents proud (and okay with the fact that they spent a small fortune on my college education). As the years after undergrad started to add up, and I was still in a dead-end job as an administrative assistant, I started to realize that my job was making me miserable. As I realized how important it is to be happy in a job, my thoughts again turned to teaching. I still loved kids, I still felt like I would be good at teaching, and I still had no idea what else I would do if I didn't teach. So I started looking into master's programs and thinking about going back to school."

Samantha eventually compromised her ego for the sake of her happiness (which, in the long term, made her care much less about what other people thought about her). "In college, I was so worried about having a job that impressed people even though I had no clue what that job would be," she says. "To me, my early to mid-twenties have been about letting go of some of the undefined, unrealistic expectations of my teens. As I realized how important caring about my job would be for my general happiness, I let go of less important, superficial concerns regarding social and economic status. Teaching will be a good fit for me, which makes me feel happier and more secure in my future than I've felt for a long time."

Finding a Passion

Penny and Devon were fortunate in that at least they knew what they were passionate about. They just had to allow themselves to get to the point where they could do what made them happy. For many twenty-somethings, this period of self-discovery is marked by myriad attempts to learn exactly what they are passionate about in the first place—a process that can take years.

For Tracy, a second lieutenant in the United States Army who graduated in 1994 from Princeton University, the twenties are "about trying scary things and taking calculated risks. After an experience, I reflect on it to figure out what I liked and didn't like." She extends this modus operandi as a way to figure out her passions. "I know there are certain things that I love and that make me feel energized instead of drained. Whenever one of those moments happens, I remember it and try to see how it fits into what I want to do in the future," she says. "Then I try to repeat it. Ultimately, all of that will come together as a vocation."

Robin, a Lincoln, Nebraska native who will get a master's degree from New York University in 2001, has a similar outlook. "Figuring out what makes you passionate is no easy feat," she says. "I still try to figure out all the different things that make me hoot for joy. If I were to list them all, it would be a hodgepodge with no rhyme or reason. But that is the key aspect that sets me aside from other people—my stamp of individuality. Your passions constantly evolve according to new experiences and new encounters."

But finding those things that energize, that make a usually staid twentysomething's heart leap, is not always easy. In fact, in the months after graduation, it is difficult to imagine settling on anything. It is for this reason that Erin, a 23-year-old student at the Colorado State University School of Veterinary Medicine (Fort Collins), suggests that in order to find true passion, graduates need to reflect on a period of life that was settled enough that they had the time, energy, and confidence to know what they liked.

"Kurt Vonnegut once wrote something about how the only way to find true happiness is through the fulfillment of childhood dreams. Now, I'm not sure how serious he was (you know that Kurt Vonnegut), but sometimes I feel as though I've made my career choice based on that premise," Erin says. "Ever since I was five years old I wanted to be a veterinarian, and now I find myself in vet school with two years left before they turn me loose. I can't say that I haven't had doubts, and I tried to get as much exposure to veterinary medicine as I could before making this commitment, but I know that I'm happy with my choice right now. I think that's really all you can do for yourself—that is, be happy with what you are doing or heading toward doing right now. I can't say that in ten or twenty years I'll still want to be a veterinarian. But I truly believe that our childhood interests say a great deal about who we are: these interests are present within us without the prejudices and stigmas that we all take into account later in life."

It is important to note that many twentysomethings, like Erin, are openminded enough to know that their passions might change and that they will have to alter their lives accordingly. "Although I realize we must all make sacrifices, I hope I never feel like all of my choices in life have been made, used up," she says. "I want to know that my life can change whenever I want it to, and I believe that it should in order to keep me enthusiastic. Perhaps 'secure' would be a good word choice to describe what I would like my future to be like. I want to know that the chances of my waking up one morning with no job, family, friends, money, or future is very slim. Perhaps this is still a lot to ask."

Keeping the Faith

When everything else around them seems to become unhinged during the shift from school to the real world, some twentysomethings turn to one of the few solid rocks in their lives for help. By leaning on religion as a vehicle for introspection, some recent graduates find they can usually ease their transition. "My religion greatly helped me in defining my identity and it has been the path that I return to whenever my self-concept is shaken," says David, a 2000 graduate of York College (Pennsylvania). "I feel that I've been fortunate in knowing who I am and what I want out of life. Along with Judaism, my identity as an artist has shaped my world view and life perceptions. These two important aspects of myself led me to choose a career as an art therapist. Art therapy allows me to share the gift of creativity with people who are in need of emotional and spiritual healing. It is the perfect blend of my spiritual notions of the world and my belief in the power of art."

For 22-year-old Andrea, from Portland, Oregon, religion provides a part of her identity that she doesn't have to worry about discovering. Her relationship with her religion is, to her comfort and relief, something that she feels will simply never change. "For the past few years, my life has, I think, been characterized by desperate last-ditch efforts to escape from modern freedom: from the (mandatory) opportunity to discover what I 'really think' about things, from the requirement to listen to my 'inner voice,' from the rule that I learn to live my life on my own," she says. "When I was a freshman in college, this search ultimately brought me to an encounter with God, and my life has never been the same since. I had been brought up attending church, and I don't want to belittle that, because I think that it had a lot to do with where I am today. But after the experience I became much more serious and purposeful in my faith. I discovered that the narrative of God's love for God's people reveals a very different kind of freedom: the freedom to never again have to worry about whether I really am somebody, because the living creator of the universe says that I am. The freedom to know what story I'm a part of and to whom I ultimately owe allegiance. The freedom to do things that are hard and promise little in the way of material success or recognition, because I know that material success and recognition don't determine my worth."

Trial and Error

It is one thing for twentysomethings to figure out who they really are by experiencing some sort of revelation, whether they reach this epiphany because they love their lives or hate them. It is quite another thing for the twentysomethings who instead bumble along, apathetically surviving, but without extreme ups or downs, until they happen to stumble across something that feels right, that they can cling to. Hoping to encounter serendipity, some recent graduates subscribe to the simple hit-or-miss theory: that the only way they will find out what matters to them most has to be through trial and error. (We should also point out here that while many twentysomethings claim they don't want to define themselves by their careers, nearly all of the ones we spoke to still responded to questions about their identities by talking about their jobs.)

Like Samantha, Justine, a 1997 graduate of the University of Utah (Salt Lake City), knew she wanted to work with children and families, but she wasn't sure whether she wanted to enter the education field (despite the summer vacations). After graduation, she decided to try a job in a completely different area. She worked for a mortgage company, got some business experience, and soon learned that she wasn't interested in becoming a businesswoman, either. So she went back to her roots: she got her master's degree in family studies, which provides a sociological perspective for studying diverse family populations. Her career possibilities now include creating and evaluating different programs for low- and middle-income families, such as Head Start, and working in the area of policy for families. Will she pursue those possibilities? She doesn't know yet. "But I chose that area just because I wasn't sure where I wanted to go," she says.

A lot of twentysomethings at least have some similarly vague idea of what they want to do with their lives, whether it is a job, a hobby, or a lifestyle. Then they use the trial-and-error method to find the precise fit for their strengths and tastes. Steve, a 22-year-old from Omaha, articulates a different perspective: he is relying on trial and error in the largest sense of the method because, like many of his peers, he has absolutely no clue what to do with himself. "I seem to have this problem: I keep bouncing from project to project or activity to activity," he says. "I think that I do not want to be mediocre. I want to be special. I know that I have talents. It is just a matter of finding that right blend of activities that challenges me on all planes—physical, spiritual, and mental. I want a job that is challenging and uses my skills. I hope that my job will turn out to be something that I can be passionate about. If not, then I will look to extracurricular activities. And I will keep searching until I find what trips my trigger: fencing, kayaking, gymnastics, dance . . . I think that we as human beings are missing something, kind of like an old man in a nursing home who is looking for his glasses and they are on his forehead."

Besides the obvious translation of Steve's metaphor, that sometimes twentysomethings can't see that the answers to their problems are right in front of them, there is also the suggestion that, eventually, twentysomethings will happen upon what they seek. That is what happened to Liz, a 29-year-old in New York who is a successful example of someone who found her calling through trial and error. After college, she planned to go backpacking in Europe for a while. During her senior year, she panicked because she didn't want to leave the country without having a job lined up, so she took the first one she found. When Liz returned from Europe, she began the "really awful job." She spent the workdays counting the hours until she could leave, and losing confidence in her abilities because her boss viewed her as very young and treated her that way. "Looking back, it was extremely stupid to take a job just to have a job, but there's a lot of anxiety during the last couple months of school, especially if you are a liberal arts major and aren't going to work for a consulting firm because you didn't study engineering," she says. "If you don't have a path laid out, you feel a lot of guilt after college because you've had this great education and you have to prove to yourself and your parents that it wasn't all for naught; beyond expanding and becoming a richer person, you hope that you also can get a job. I was one of five people under 35, so we didn't have anything to talk about. I was lonely, and I didn't eat very much, which is a pattern if I'm not happy."

From the start of her eight-month stint, she was looking for another job. She constantly sent résumés to big public relations firms but didn't get any responses. She even applied to graduate school because she didn't know what else she should be doing. Finally, she got an interview. "I didn't think I'd want to work there because the interviewer was snotty and because I got the interview by lowering my standards," Liz says. "I applied to be an intern after working for eight months. I felt awful because I was still living at home, commuting to the city, and making the salary of an intern. It was a step back in a lot of ways. But I was suddenly working with a hundred people under 30. Some of the other interns were right out of school, so my eight months at the first job really paid off. I was only an intern for four weeks instead of twelve because I was so good. So they offered me the chance to drive cross-country and be a media spokesperson for a major ad campaign."

By the time Liz returned from the campaign, she had learned a lot about herself. She is content now with her career, but she figures that because trial and error worked well for her before, it can work for her again. "I never thought I'd work for such a large corporate entity—I work for one of the largest PR agencies in the world. But I question whether what I do is intellectually challenging. I'm amused all day but not necessarily using any advanced thinking, so I sometimes get frustrated with that—feeling bored when I impress people at work when I don't think what I did was such a big deal," she says. Recently, Liz applied to law school.

Using the trial and error method doesn't always have to be a complete shot in the dark, however. In some cases, when twentysomethings allow for happenstance by staying openminded, they can get a better sense of the sorts of things they should try. Kara, a 1996 graduate of Furman University (Greenville, South Carolina), always thought she should go into a career in the field of fine arts. "I taught myself to draw and paint and it was the major focus of my high school academic life. I was inspired by everything and assumed that when I grew up, I was going to move to New York City, live by myself, and be some type of artist. So I went to college to get a Bachelor of Fine Arts degree. I was still inspired in college, but with the deadlines and the piles of other work I had to do, it just didn't feel the same. I stuck to it, though, and still envisioned the life of a graphic designer or a photographer."

After college, though, Kara decided to follow her college sweetheart back to his native Venezuela. "At that point I could not imagine following my 'dream' of going to live in New York to become an artist because it seemed too unreal," she says. "So I began teaching English in a private school in Venezuela. While I was there, it hit me: this is what I am really meant to do. I loved everything about it and realized that I had always loved teaching children at summer camp every year. When I returned to the United States with my husband (we married in Venezuela), I got a job as a preschool teacher and went back to school at the same time to become certified in elementary education. After two years and a lot of work, I am now a kindergarten teacher truly living out my dream. I love what I do and I could not imagine doing anything else. Meanwhile, I still do art as a hobby and love that there are no deadlines or pressures and that I am inspired again."

Changing Their Minds

Sometimes, instead of settling on aspects of their lives by trial and error or because they have resigned themselves to accepting some sort of compromise, twentysomethings switch things around more permanently: for whatever reason, they change their minds. Sandra, a 1997 graduate of Ohio Wesleyan University (Delaware, Ohio), changed her mind about a lot of things after she graduated, and she still questions whether or not she has chosen wisely. "Sometimes I feel totally confident and I have no worries. Other times, though, I seriously question what I'm doing with my life, where it's headed, and whether I'm wasting my time or not," she says. "I was engaged when I graduated from college, but I broke off the engagement after six months, which was an incredibly painful but necessary action. I spent the next two years ignoring any fears and doubts about myself or my life and instead just focused on having a good time. But now I've started facing all of these issues again, and I'm glad that I'm dealing with them, although it can be really depressing to look around my apartment (which is always messy) and think about what a failure I am (even though I don't really think I'm a failure)."

For twentysomethings, changing their minds is a big risk that can be accompanied by extreme fear and anxiety. As Sandra points out, it's like starting all over again. "I've finally figured out what I want to do with my life (I think), and I'm so scared that I'm going to fail at it," she says. "I always thought, at least through college, that I would get married and raise children—that's what I wanted to do with my life. And then, especially after I broke off my engagement, I faced the fact that that wasn't going to happen. And I realized that I don't want to make marriage my goal, because I'm afraid that if marriage is a goal for me, then I'll settle for some less-than-perfect man when I hit 30 just because 'the time is right.' To be honest, that's what I did in college. I met someone who seemed 'right' and I got engaged to him. But I didn't love him. And now that I've escaped that once, I'm very determined to never let it happen again, so I never expect to be married. So it's hard because I feel I need to balance the want with the need, to make sure I don't settle. I hope not. I have a backup plan: if I'm not married at 30, I'll buy a cat (I already have two). And then if I'm still single at 35, I'll buy another cat. And then, if I'm still single at 40, I'll buy another cat, which means my goal in life is this: at the age of 40, I'll either be married or have five cats.

"Regarding the rest of my life, I've never been a big planner, you know, with the five-year plans and goals," Sandra continues. "I tend to just let my life unfold and stay open-minded about what opportunities come before me. I don't think there'll ever be a time when my whole life is settled, and I'm kind of glad. To be honest, that's what's best about the twenties—we're so free. No mortgages, no kids, no job that we've been at for fifteen years. The problem, though, as I've tried to explain a million times to my mom, is that freedom is really a big burden. When all the options are available, it's really easy to sit on your butt and choose nothing. I was like that for a long time—three years, I guess. I ended up in a great computer job, which I really enjoyed for two years. But recently I've realized that I want to be in another field, and now I have to start all over again. However, it's great to actually have something in my life that I'm certain of. The uncertainty can kill you."

Some twentysomethings take comfort in the fact that they can change their minds more easily now, when they have fewer responsibilities, with fewer repercussions. Jack, a 1995 graduate of Lehigh University (Bethlehem, Pennsylvania), enjoys his job, likes the people he works with, makes a good salary, and goes to school on his company's dime. The job is ideal for him right now, but he doesn't plan on staying with the company—or even the industry—for too long. "I think about leaving all the time, especially if the stock takes off," he says. "I could become a musician, or do something else. I don't look at myself as being in the computer industry for years, because I never really loved computers all that much, but it is a great way to support myself and my other habits. I don't mind it, because it's mathematical and logical, but I'd like to teach; I've always enjoyed tutoring people. It's a nice feeling, maybe because it makes me feel smarter than other people. Or I'd be a camp counselor. I enjoy being outside, moving around. I hate sitting still, and this job certainly involves sitting still. I don't think there are many jobs that people go out and love. My outlook now is that if I can go to work, not mind it, and enjoy myself to some extent, my hobbies and personal life are how I live my life. My current job is the way I will be able to afford to enjoy the rest of my life."

Job-Hopping

One major difference between twentysomethings now and twenty-somethings thirty years ago is that, in terms of jobs, recent graduates in the twenty-first century can change their minds more quickly, more often, and more easily. (This is, of course, a double-edged sword: the increase in options at any given time gives young adults more choices, sure, but it means they have more decisions to make, as discussed in Chapter 5.) While traditional, old-style career guides advise young professionals to stay in each job at least nine months to a year, the country is in the midst of a very different job market than in past generations. Although it is not the best way to establish a solid track record, twenty-somethings are increasingly realizing that job-hopping does not have as damaging a stigma as it did even a decade ago. Job-hopping is now such a common trend that, for many employers, it has become an acceptable one. What this means for young graduates is that they always have an out. "I am a temp on a trading floor. It's not my ideal job, but I'm learning. Do I want to become permanent? Yes. Do I want a better job? You bet. But there are no quick fixes," says Rick, a 1997 graduate of the University of Wisconsin–Madison. "I enjoy this stupid job somehow. I know a lot about finance now, and that will help me to get into economic development and other goals. They are building blocks. And I know it's temporary—I'll be here for nine months max, then find something else. I want to try about three to five different fields. After that I will feel confident that I'll be doing what I like—filling both my pockets and mind."

At the same time, some twentysomethings worry that the knowledge that they can leave their jobs at any time and still get another one might be something they could take advantage of—and raise their standards too high in the process. If they have to fight boredom at one job, they might encounter boredom at the next job. They fear falling into a pattern of "the two-month itch," in which, after some time at one job, they will get bored and look to switch—because they can. "If you're bored, see what things excite you in your office or field that you don't do. If you're really that bored, look around internally. But if you look at people who were in your position a year or two ago and they're still bored, then it may be time to move on," Rick suggests. "Switching jobs quickly is not a bad thing, but you should make an effort to like where you are now. If it doesn't work, it doesn't work, so move on. Do not reject a job for fear of jumping ship in two months. Try it out, and if you dick over the company, so what. If *you* are not looking out for your own mental and career health, who is?"

Twentysomethings should expect boredom as an inevitable part of the first stages of a career, says Derrick, a 1993 graduate of James Madison University (Harrisonburg, Virginia). "You might be bored at your job. You probably will be. When you first get out of college, it's mandated that you have a very boring job," he says. "Just remember that you're young and you won't be there for the rest of your life. The important thing is that you're making money and supporting yourself. You should try to stay at any given job for at least a year. After a year, it's okay to go."

Robin, from Lincoln, Nebraska, says that job-hopping is merely a method of trial and error that allows twentysomethings to narrow down their fields of choice. "My dad always says, 'Look at me. I am 58 and I still have not yet found an ideal job that I absolutely love through and through. So I try different things until I find something that I am good at and that I enjoy. I have been doing this for years, and chances are that you too will experience several different careers and job experiences before you find something that you truly enjoy. It might take six months, it might take two years, it might take twelve years. But there is something out there exactly for you, and until you run into that perfect fit, you try out several different venues and figure out what you don't like.' I have found this to be the truest advice," she says. "I have been out of college for one year, working in the business world, and I've discovered that there are many aspects of it that are just not for me. So I have decided to go back for my master's in French studies. Exactly what I will do with that degree remains to be seen, but it is something that I truly enjoy and would love to be able to incorporate into my daily working life afterwards."

Although the process of changing their minds can create even more havoc for recent graduates who are already going through a harrowing time, it often teaches them something about themselves. "Growing up—don't ask me why—I really wanted to be someone out of *Thirtysomething*," says Meredith, a 1996 graduate of Colby College (Waterville, Maine). "Sure, they had their problems (a lot of problems) but they were living well, doing well, had great jobs, were total yuppies— and I wanted to be like that. Especially the successful yuppie part."

When it was time to decide on a major, however, she just couldn't fulfill her dream of yuppiedom by going into economics or accounting.

So instead she graduated with a degree in speech communications. Before Thanksgiving of her senior year, Meredith landed a job at one of the top consulting companies in the country—a position she held for four years. "Did I make a lot of money? Pretty much. Did I have meetings with CEOs and COOs and other VIPs? Sure did. Did I get to go to shi-shi restaurants and bars to impress recruits? Of course. Was I fulfilled? Not at all," she says. "I realized just over a year ago that I was not really helping anyone. The world could certainly go on if I didn't reorganize the way the Billing and AR department of Client X runs, or train the entire staff of Company Y. In fact, five hundred people might still have jobs if I hadn't elected to enter the factors and variables I saw fit into a staffing plan. But heaven help me, that is all I did. I realized this at a very pivotal point in my life. I had also just learned that my roommate was moving out, the relationship I'd been in for about two years ended, and my grandfather fell ill," she says.

When she arrived at this point in her twenties, when all of her borders felt like they were falling in, she didn't know what was going on. "I was not having problems with alcohol or keeping food down, so I didn't really think I needed a counselor. Yet any time I let myself think, I literally started to shake," she says. "And then I was asked a question that really helped me put a lot of things into perspective. I was asked, 'What do you want people in your life to be saying about you when you're 80?' I had to look beyond my immediate confusion and focus on my future. I thought about how I had come to where I am, how everything that had seemed so important once upon a time seemed silly to me now, and that really worried me."

After mulling over her priorities for a while, Meredith decided that if, upon reflection, she wasn't both proud of and fulfilled by her job, then it was not a job worth having. So she decided to change directions completely. "My résumé will not be my eulogy. My friends and family will be speaking about what I meant to them. So, when I'm 80, I realized, I'll want to be thought of as a warm and loving person, a good listener and empathizer, a person whom my friends and family turn to for support in the bad times and for laughs in the good ones. If I am going to do that, I have to find a way to spend my time in a way that allows me to remain who I am. I need to find a career that will allow me to utilize the same energies that I use in being a friend and relative now."

Confronting her identity crisis head-on gave Meredith the insight to figure out why she was unhappy, as well as the guts to start all over again. Eventually she applied to graduate school. She is currently a graduate student at Harvard University, where she plans to get a master's degree in education. "It was my little 25-year-old epiphany. But that little question really made me focus," she says. "Going forward, I will always keep in mind the person I want to be known as when I'm 80—and I hope that will always ensure that I continue to be true to who I am now, and who I want to be later."

Constant Evolution

Much of the stress of being a twentysomething is about trying to settle various aspects of life, whether it's a career (that's usually the big one), romance, social life, or living arrangements (more on balancing all of these in Chapter 6). In their attempts to reconcile who they are with who they want to be, recent graduates sometimes go through what seems like an interminable hunt for what makes them happy. It is a difficult process, but one of the reasons it is so tough is because twentysomethings are trying to figure out several goals and then attain them all at once, as if once they have gotten to the end of every path they can imagine for themselves, they will find true happiness. But maybe that's the problem.

Many twentysomethings, like Phil, a 25-year-old native of New Orleans, say they plan to keep changing their lives because they are scared of falling into a tedious monotony. "I've often thought, how much longer can I really do this? Is it something I'm going to do for the rest of my life? I don't think so but I'm really comfortable at it so I don't know what it will take to shake me out of that," Phil says. "What if I want to go back to school and become a lawyer or something? I don't know when I'll want to do that because I'm so happy now. But there is reason for change. What I do now I'm really happy at, but I worry that it will not excite me anymore. In four or five years I think I will get burnt out. Even people our parents' age are now switching career fields. I want to switch fields in a couple of years because I would see it as another challenge and I'd want to pursue that. I think it's part of what makes us vibrant—finding new opportunities."

This is a view that is often overlooked. Twentysomethings are a constantly evolving species, so maybe it isn't all about reaching the end of a path, but rather about the twists and turns along the way. As Jeff said in the beginning of this chapter, the day that everything is settled in a life could very well be the end of it. Indeed, the process of self discovery can be a goal in itself: instead of always looking ahead to the point where parts of their identities are resolved, maybe some twentysomethings say, they should relax, because it is during this time of resolving their identities that they may be the most attuned to themselves. In fact, maybe twentysomethings could be just as well off by never really figuring themselves out, because searching for answers and continually finding challenges is what drives their lives and gives them a sense of purpose.

Mike, a 1995 graduate of George Washington University (Washington, D.C.) who went straight from college to Emory Law School (Atlanta), says that because his goals are constantly changing, figuring himself out is a continuous process. After he graduated from law school, he moved to a new city and was immediately faced with three obstacles: studying for the bar, adjusting to life in a new city, and finding a job. The bar was initially his most pressing concern. As for everything else, he says, it was a matter of waiting things out, and hoping, and working for everything to fall into place. He had a vague idea of what he wanted to do, but he felt he had to work hard to make that idea a reality. "So basically, I learned how to depend on myself a lot more than ever before, because in college and law school, there was a set agenda, a set way to meet people, to figure out what your agenda was going to be like," he says. "And when I was done studying for the bar, it was up to me to make that all happen. There wasn't a set curriculum to follow for the first time. So you learn to be patient. I've always been a dreamer, so I had a dream in mind, but in terms of making it into reality, that was another story. And I believe that if you work hard enough, things do fall into place; you just can't always control the timing of when or how these things happen. I had to do a few other things on the way, in the process of finding, for example, the job I wanted to be at. I realized that even if you have this master plan of where you want to be, in reality you realize that until you're there experiencing it, you don't know what you're getting into. I still feel like I'm striving toward these goals, but in the process of learning what makes me happy and what I want to be, the goals have changed."

When twentysomethings are going through this identity crisis, things can seem overly complex and chaotic. Mario, a 1998 graduate of Tufts University (Medford, Massachusetts), suggests that if recent graduates would merely simplify their process of self-discovery with a motto like "get happy," their transitions into the real world would be much more bearable. Because of this attitude, Mario says that figuring out who he really is has been a fairly uncomplicated process. "I know what I want to do and what I don't want to do," he says. "At times we have to compromise; however, people too often compromise themselves. I just try to do whatever will make me happier, and think of myself first (kind of self-centered, huh?). But if more people did it, they would be happier. I'd like to put this in context to make myself seem like less of an idiot. Don't take a job because it pays more and would make your parents happy or impress your friends. Take it because it is what you want to do, or if the money makes you happy, great. If you don't feel like going out on a weekend night, don't." And perhaps Mario's most crucial piece of advice: "Don't worry about what others think."

It seems simple to say, but that's the point—and it's a creed that many twentysomethings find difficult to follow. The process of self-discovery begins and ends with the self. So by trying to focus solely on their own happiness, as Mario advises, twentysomethings can begin to define their identities more quickly and more clearly. Twentysomethings know the slogans: "Just be." "Just do it." (Note to Calvin Klein and Nike: We are available immediately for promotional spots.) Maybe another appropriate one would be "Just live."

two
What If I'm Scared to Stop Being a Kid?

R emember recess? What a terrific concept—a regularly scheduled playtime that was fully stocked with friends, playground equipment, a nefarious Recess Lady, and the all-important red rubber bouncy balls. Whatever happened to that? Most companies have yet to realize that if they would just institute an optional recess time—maybe not right after lunch, as elementary schools schedule it (how we managed to tear around on the jungle gym immediately after snarfing down the cafeteria's mystery bean chili on cheesy toast, we will never know), but at, say, three P.M.—employees would be happier, more productive, and more physically fit. Sure, we've heard about the tech companies where employees spontaneously break into Nerf games, or take an occasional field trip to the nearest paintball setup. On the whole, however, most employers don't even think to incorporate recess into the workday.

But recess symbolizes a lot of what made us happy as children: carefree abandon, unstructured play, reckless endangerment (anyone who never had to go see the nurse because of a recess "incident" probably never really had a true recess experience). Granted, there might have been some playground politics, but generally we were more interested in playtime than protocol. Recess signified childhood, and childhood was, generally, magical, even if we didn't realize it back then. Our parents took care of our responsibilities, and we didn't worry about what we looked like, or what we ate, or whom we pleased, or if we were going to be successful. We just were. And we were happy that way.

Think about it—everything we did back then was so simple. How did we spend our days? We watched *Scooby-Doo,* even though it always had the same ending. We traded stuff, whether it was cards (Pac Man, Garbage Pail, baseball), stickers, gummy bracelets, or Transformers. We ate our peanut-butter-and-jelly sandwiches cut into triangles with the crusts cut off, and we didn't have to do the cutting. We poked at our cafeteria food with plastic sporks. In the summer, we did headstands in the swimming pool. In the winter, we went sledding down the ubiquitous "Suicide Hill." Whatever the season, we played in dirt. And sometimes ate it.

We aren't actually going to write one of those full-on "Children of the Eighties" types of essays. Other people have already cornered that market pretty well. Furthermore, this book should also apply to children of the nineties and on—some of whom will know cartoons like *Cow and Chicken* but will have no idea what a Smurf is. But the reason that twentysomethings like to read those kinds of reflections is because it reminds them of a time when nothing really mattered too much. When something did matter, it affected them one way or another, and then they moved on without looking back. Those little wisps of nostalgia recall a simpler time that a lot of twentysomethings associate with happiness. Often they try to recapture that period, even just for a moment. Sometimes they are successful and sometimes they aren't. But when their failures to recapture their childhood outnumber the successes, they start to get scared and they wonder if they have lost it for good.

Do they ever?

Devon, a 1998 graduate of Cornell University (Ithaca, New York), says the idea of no longer being a kid terrifies her. "Being a kid is such a huge part of who I am. I am convinced that what is wrong with the majority of the world today is that it's full of grown-ups," she says. "Recently, while on the treadmill at the gym, I realized how stupid the whole thing is—how grown-ups spend so much money to sweat in small, germ-infested rooms on bizarre equipment just to get exercise when all they really need to do is play more. When was the last time you or any other 'grown-up' you know went out to play during a lunch break?"

Devon has actually tried to retain her childhood by clinging desperately to that last bastion of unabashed playtime. "Being a teacher, I look at all of the kids out at recess, shooting hoops, jumping rope, and running around while all of the teachers sit on their asses and eat (myself included)," she says. "I have never really been overly athletic, though I'm probably more so now than ever before, but one day I did do something about it. I actually went outside during my lunch period and 'played' with the kids. I attempted to shoot some hoops with the boys for a bit. Then, when my lack of coordination was proving too evident, I joined some of the girls at what looked like a simple game of jump rope, but later I found out was double Dutch. (Um, I had fun nonetheless.) The other teachers thought I was nuts—this I'm used to—but the kids were psyched. Hmm. Maybe I'll do it again tomorrow."

Undoubtedly, recess is easier for Devon than for other twentysomethings because it is automatically built into her day as a teacher. But her general philosophy certainly is not limited to people who are in the education profession. As a teacher, she may have more opportunities than other recent graduates to remember what being a child is like, but as a twentysomething, Devon, like many of her peers, wants to keep those memories vivid—and, on occasion, still apply them to her adult life. "I'm convinced that people take themselves way too seriously in life. I'm not quite sure when this starts—I think sometime around now, when real life stresses start to build, like money, finances, jobs, relationships," she says. "Grown-ups miss out on some of the best things because they walk right by them. I try so hard to keep the child within alive and well. I'm fortunate because I am surrounded by children. Watching their self-discovery is amazing and reminds me on a daily basis to do the same. To tell you the truth, most of the time I feel like this whole young-adult thing is a hoax. That sooner or later they're all going to catch on and find out that I'm not really a grown-up, and man, will I be in trouble then. But for now, I think I've got most of them fooled."

As Devon suggests, one reason twentysomethings cling to their childhood is because they don't want to lose their free-spiritedness. Others say that because their identities were formed as children, to grow out of childhood means to lose much of their sense of self.

Shane, a 23-year-old living in Knoxville, Tennessee, says that another reason twentysomethings are afraid to stop being kids is that they want to maintain the benefits and societal perks that inevitably come with appearances of youthfulness. From a commercial standpoint, particularly, this view makes sense. Youth is vibrant. Youth sells. But Shane points out that regaining youth also means reliving the past, which complicates the way twentysomethings relate to their childhood.

Shane cites several physical explanations for why people wish they could be younger. He mentions the graying hair, the receding hairline, the expanding waistline, the drooping breasts, the hair growing and falling out of the wrong places all as natural reasons to wish to be younger. But if people really could travel back to the years when they didn't have to worry about these physical problems, they would also be traveling back to a time when they didn't have the knowledge or experience necessary to appreciate that the problems haven't yet occurred. That, Shane says, is where twentysomethings are: they are starting to fear those problems but do not yet appreciate that they don't really have to worry about them quite yet. The twenties are a time of conflicting self-image—an image compounded by twentysomethings' competing desires to look backward and move forward at the same time. "There are so many times I look at myself in the mirror and I think my body's going to shit. But then I have to remind myself that I'm only in my twenties. If I think that now, how am I going to perceive myself when I'm 30, or how about 40?" he says. "I also think back to when I didn't care about these things, or rather didn't appreciate them, and I wish for a moment that I could. But when I realize how much I didn't know or was naive about, I don't think it would be a fair trade. In fact, I think I would take the knowledge over the physical attributes. Maybe it's a sign of my maturing, or maybe I've just gotten sick of worrying. Regardless, I know I can't reverse the aging process and there's no sense in hating every moment of it. How happy would I be?"

Shane used to date a girl who was the type of person who tried to fight aging as much as she could. He says that one of the things that turned him off about her was that for months she dreaded turning 20 years old because she was afraid of losing her childhood by biologically becoming an official twentysomething. "Frankly, I think there are a lot bigger problems to worry about," Shane says. "I mean, if anything, she was in the prime physical years of her life. To me, if she's afraid to turn 20, she's afraid to venture out and do anything on her own. I understand that it's a pseudo-milestone, two decades of life. I remember when I turned 10, I tried to get a bigger present from my mom for that birthday, reasoning that it was the first decade of my life and it was the only time I would turn ten (it didn't work). But at 20, life is just beginning. It seems like she saw her life as ending." Largely because of the disparate ways they viewed their young-adult years, Shane and his girlfriend broke up soon after her twentieth birthday. But the girl's fear of her twenties is hardly uncommon.

End of the Innocence

Several recent graduates point to specific moments during their twenty-something years when they realized that they had pretty much stopped being kids and instead had gotten past the embarkation stage of adulthood. Often these moments coincide with firsts—first apartment, first long-term romance, first job. Tanya, a 1996 graduate of the University of Vermont (Burlington), says that she first felt like an adult soon after graduation. "I remember the moment when I felt like I wasn't a kid anymore," she says. "When I was 23, I moved into my own apartment. The first time I listened to my refrigerator hum, I got this fleeting thing in my stomach. This was my refrigerator in my apartment. Sometime that first week, I remember getting up in the middle of the night to go to the bathroom and I got really excited because it was my own bathroom." (Sometimes it doesn't take much.)

While those moments can feel empowering at times, they can also spark a fear of adulthood and an anxiety over leaving life as kids know it behind. "Occasionally when I'm on a crowded subway at rush hour," Tanya says, "I'll step back and think to myself, 'This is my life for the next fifty years, this is what I do, this is real, this is never going to end'—and that's a little scary. Hitting 25 wasn't fun. It felt like I was almost 30. Where did it all go?"

Notably, Tanya adds that she won't feel entirely like she is an adult until she has children of her own. This feeling represents a common view among twentysomethings: that childhood doesn't end until they are responsible for someone else's childhood. Jesse, a 1992 graduate of Alfred University (New York), explains that twentysomething parenthood is so much of a responsibility that it forces young people to grow up. "I had a kid when I was 29. It changes things," he says. "When you get married, you have someone else you're responsible for, but that person can take care of herself. When you have a kid, though, you have this little helpless thing. If it's up, you have to stay up, even if you want to go to sleep. If it's hungry, you have to get it food. Being a father was weird at first, but you have time to get used to it—it's not like you have a kid and it comes out and says 'Dad,' like when you get married and have to immediately refer to your 'wife.'"

This strange adjustment period, other young parents say, at the same time also means that having a kid doesn't necessarily signify a sudden end of childhood. Laura, a 29-year-old from Louisville, Kentucky, says that having a child at first made her act like one. "I felt like more of a kid when I had my baby. All of a sudden you feel helpless, you have no idea what you're doing, and you're calling your mom every five minutes to ask for help," she says.

Jesse wasn't immediately thrust from childhood to adulthood as soon as he became a father, however. Instead, his transition occurred over a number of years during a series of changes that caused him to grow up. "In college, I lived with three guys in an apartment that was a pit, and went out drinking beer every night," he says. "Then I graduated and during my first year of law school I was living with my girlfriend in an apartment. We had our own stuff. We didn't have all of our college friends around anymore, so that part of life was cut off a little bit. But in some ways it was like my girlfriend and I were only playing house—it didn't feel completely real. It was like playing an adult, but I didn't really feel like an adult. It was too early for us to be living together like that. So I moved to Phoenix by myself. I got a car, drove cross-country, and moved into my own apartment alone. I didn't know anybody; I didn't have any friends in Phoenix. I was on my own and I didn't have anybody to rely on but myself. Once I knew I could do it, that made me realize that I could get married and be an adult for real."

For some twentysomethings, the moments when they realize they no longer think of themselves as children come unexpectedly and often. Nina, a 23-year-old Seattle resident, says her evolution into adulthood is marked with regular reminders that her life is changing and she can't stop that. "In my case, it happens at least once every day," she says. "Sometimes, I realize it when I wake up in the morning in my own apartment and make my coffee. Or while I'm changing in the dressing room at a clothing store. Or watching the school play at my old high school. Or checking my voice mail at work. Or going home to my parents' house. Or sipping a vodka sour at the edge of a bar, talking to some 30-year-old lawyer, and wanting to ask him if he caught the last episode of *The Real World*. Or at a concert, passing a joint to the kid next to me and wondering, 'What the hell am I doing here?—I have a nine-o'clock meeting tomorrow morning.' It will happen when you least expect it. I think that it is okay to fear those moments as long as you derive some sort of comfort from them, as well. Getting older is an inescapable process. It is happening now as you read this. If we constantly fear the inevitable, we will never really live. Those moments when I find myself pausing, taking stock of what's around me and how far I have come, are bittersweet; I feel sad because I am getting old and I can never go back and relive anything again, yet that same sadness is mitigated because I am getting older and never have to go back and relive anything. You should never beat yourself up for fearing that moment when you realize you are no longer a kid."

According to Nina, twentysomethings shouldn't dread that intangible time when, suddenly, it dawns on them that they are no longer children. One reason is that, as she suggests, there probably will not be one single, definable moment that divides life into pre-"moment" (twentysomething as child) and post-"moment" (twentysomething as adult). Another reason is that if people spend their lives dreading the next big change, then there is a good chance they will spend far too many of the years to come fixating on this fear.

The transition between childhood and adulthood is as much about confusion as it is about fear. The dichotomy of living in two vastly different worlds at the same time and trying to morph them into one leaves recent graduates uncertain about which mind-set to prioritize. Olivia, a

2000 graduate of Dalhousie University (Halifax, Nova Scotia), says this limbo leaves her with questions that she hasn't yet learned how to answer. "In certain respects, I am excited to stop being a kid. I want to pay for everything myself. I come from a wealthy background, so many things have been provided for me," she says. "I am happy that for the first time in my life, I will only spend what I earn. Things may be tough, especially if I work a low-paying nonprofit job in high-cost San Francisco. But it will be a learning experience, and I'll just be so happy to be independent."

On the other hand, Olivia says, she still finds it strange when people regard her as an adult because, like other recent graduates, she isn't sure what adulthood truly means. Because Olivia associates being an adult with having to stifle, censor, and tame herself, she doesn't particularly want to be one. "I often strive to preserve the childlike side of my personality," she says. "For instance, for my graduation, I affixed a couple of small Bert and Ernie toys to my mortarboard. I think it is significant that on the day of my passage into the adult world, I had children's TV characters on my cap. I suppose I am frightened of adulthood because in many ways it seems to represent the end of fun. Not only am I not ready to stop having fun, but I am not ready to stop having the *young* kind of fun. Sure, I like the symphony and the theater. But I also, frankly, like to drink and smoke. I like to dance all night to techno music. I like to flirt, hook up, fall in love. I cannot resist the appeal of a moon bounce. When will I have to stop doing these things? I hope it will be never; but such activities seem unseemly in a 45-year-old. So where do I draw the line? Does the end of college mean the end of fun?"

Are We There Yet?

Another dimension that can make the twenties dissipate the line between childhood and adulthood into a hazy blur involves not only the ways that twentysomethings think of themselves, but also the ways

What If I'm Scared to Stop Being a Kid?

that other people treat them. At exactly the time when some twenty-somethings are trying to segue into adulthood, the people in their lives often still categorize them as children. Amanda, a 24-year-old from Little Rock, Arkansas, experiences this treatment at her current job as a researcher at an economic consulting firm. "I thought I would like working with a bunch of young people, but it also turned out to be bad because then we're like the kids downstairs. We don't get many responsibilities because we're all thought of as lesser people rather than equal coworkers at another company," she says. Because her superiors view Amanda as a kid, they don't give her responsibilities worthy of an adult. As a result, her on-the-job morale suffers. "The job's been okay and I like my coworkers, but the work is boring and half the time I don't have work to do. I don't like feeling like a lackey for the economists—they just call you when they need something," she says.

Other twentysomethings agree with Amanda that the upsides of working with several other twentysomethings inevitably can be accompanied by the disadvantage of being lumped together as a group of kids. Brandon, a 24-year-old living in Los Angeles, works as one of twenty-five pages at a network studio. On one hand, he says, he loves the collegiate atmosphere. "I know a lot of people our age who get their first jobs, work with older people, and feel separated from everybody else. But here everyone's the same age, give or take five years, and everyone wants to do something big in the entertainment industry, so we all have instantaneous compatibility. Once or twice a week and once on weekends we all hang out at somebody's house or at a bar. It's great," he says. "But it's twofold."

Although the twentysomething environment makes the transition from college to the real world a little bit easier, Brandon points out that it also makes it more difficult to feel like an adult. "It's sort of like a pre-job job," he says. "Working as a page, we have to wear uniforms, which is the dead giveaway. It's not even a question of exactly how old you are. You're labeled. They know you're just out of college. What makes it worse is that almost everyone else beside the pages is distinctly older than we are. So they look at us and think not only that we're young but also that we're idiots. It's not necessarily their fault—some of us *are* idiots. But they have this attitude that because we're young, we don't know what life is like and we just don't know anything, period. Because of the uniforms, we don't even get to pretend that we're adults. If you're there four, six, eight months, you can't wait to get out of that polyester uniform. It can be degrading. It's like everyone is wearing a freshman T-shirt."

The Parent Trap

One of the most challenging shifts between childhood and adulthood is the changing relationship with parents. The familial link never disappears, of course—your parents will always be your parents and you will always be their child. But in the days after graduation, a twenty-something slowly comes to realize that the playing field has leveled to a certain extent because there is no longer that "Me Adult, You Kid" separation. Well, not as much of one, anyway. To complicate the relationship even more, now that twentysomethings are out of school, they may work alongside people their parents' age; they might go drinking with people their parents' age; they might supervise people their parents' age; and in some cases, they may even date people their parents' age. As a result, twentysomethings eventually come to see their parents as—whoa—people. And that can be a weird feeling.

Twenty-two-year-old Andrea, from Portland, Oregon, started dating a man more than twice her age less than a year after she graduated from college. They connected as what she calls an "ageless" couple; although her boyfriend was, at 51, only five months younger than her father, Andrea quickly forgot about the age difference as the pair found more and more things in common. But although she considered herself an independent adult, Andrea still believed she had to run the relationship by her parents for approval. "I knew that if I were to begin dating him, my parents might well disapprove. So I asked them," she says. "They weren't crazy about the idea, although they did concede that he sounded like a wonderful person, but said they would reserve judgment for the time being. I'm grateful for their willingness to take my feelings into account."

However, if Andrea's parents had categorically disapproved of the relationship, or if they decide to disapprove at any time in the future, Andrea says she would defy her friends' advice to follow her heart and instead honor her parents' request. "Many people, I think, would suggest that my mentality reveals a lack of maturity on my part," she says. "That if I were 'really' an adult, I would be able to discover what I 'really think' is right, apart from the influence of my parents. The problem with these people's understanding of freedom is that when what I 'really think'—which, more often than not, means what immediately strikes me as comfortable—trumps everything else, I'm doomed to live in a world no bigger than my own whims. Certainly my own comfort is pretty important to me (too important, in fact), but even I realize that my own comfort—right down to my Wamsutta sheets and Gap twin set—isn't ultimately transcendent, and doesn't make sense of the universe. What does this have to do with my parents, or my decision making, or with my no longer being a kid? I think that parents—and family in general—provide one's means to true freedom. If I concede that there are some cases in which my parents may know better than I do, then I'm placing myself in a world and a story that's much bigger than myself."

The gap between childhood and adulthood grows even stranger when a recent graduate moves back home after college or graduate school. After four or more years of relative independence, moving on back to the old bedroom as an alleged adult is just plain peculiar. Suddenly, "As long as you live under my roof" becomes a factor again. At a time when a twentysomething is already struggling with leaving behind the shelter of college for the responsibilities of adulthood, living at home can spark something of a regression. The days of free pizza are left behind in favor of the days of setting the dinner table.

When Katie, a 1996 graduate of Wesleyan University (Middletown, Connecticut), moved in with her parents two years ago, she had just returned from a stint in the Peace Corps and wanted to save some money to pay for graduate school. She got along well with her mother, if not her stepfather, but both parents were eventually pretty good at leaving her alone. (It helped that she lived in the basement, where she had her own bathroom.) To contribute to the living arrangement instead of paying rent, Katie did chores and had to take responsibility for the bill of her choosing, so she paid off her younger brother's college loans. Meanwhile, she had to adjust to a compromised social life because she was living with her parents. "I didn't have parties because it was my parents' house, but my boyfriend slept over all the time. My mother was really mad about it—she told me not to have him sleep over because my stepdad felt it was inappropriate. I told her I understood her point, but I wasn't going to listen, so eventually she dropped it," she says. "My stepdad also resented the fact that I was 24 and living at home, using his car. He felt I needed to be on my own and that my mom was coddling me. My mom understood the situation people our age are in—trying to save money and live cheaply is really hard at our salary level." After a couple of years of independence in the Peace Corps, Katie felt like she was regressing because of the constant nagging. "I would ask my mom for advice about everything, but she also kept tabs on how much money I was saving, and she and my stepfather would make judgments on how I spent my money. When I went shopping they would say how extravagant I was. The time it was really hard was when I had to use their car," she says.

Devon encountered a similar feeling when she moved back in with her parents after graduation. She was hesitant to return home, but she realized that it was the best option for her at that time. Living at home made it tricky to figure out her adult identity, she says. "I was trying so damned hard to establish myself as a 'me' in society and not be one of those people who mooch off of Mom and Dad forever, although sometimes that sounds so appealing. I have wonderful parents. We get along great. Yeah, we went through that weird adolescent and teen angsty stuff, and yeah, my mom is overprotective and my dad can be way too passive for his own good sometimes, but they are my parents and I love them for it." After four years of doing, as Devon puts it, "what I wanted, how I wanted, and *who* I wanted when I wanted," the idea of reverting back to her parents' rules was hardly appealing. "But considering that my new job was less than five minutes away and that financially I hardly had a pot to piss in, Mom and Dad's place was looking good. I sucked in my pride and went home. Not that there's anything wrong with living with your parents. I just didn't want to live with mine. Living with my parents made me feel weird. I don't know exactly why—it just did."

A year and a half later, Devon decided that she could not grow fully into an adult while she was still living in the house in which she grew up as a child. So she saved some money and found a place, even though she knew that moving out would mean she would have financial hardships for the next few years. "I found a wonderful place, about a half hour from where I work. It is mine—well, not bought and paid for, mind you; rented—but from my paycheck. Everything in it was bought and paid for by me," she says. "Let me tell you, it feels good. I'm working hard to pay my own way and feel fortunate that I have the ability to do so. I am also putting myself through grad school at night little by little. This also feels good. There have been a few months that I just barely made rent, but I am doing it. Did moving out of my parents' home make sense for the long run? Probably not. And I think about it from time to time. But for now this is what I felt I needed to do to better myself. This is definitely a transition time and this is how I feel I need to make my transition: by becoming fully self supportive financially, emotionally, physically, and spiritually. I personally didn't feel that I could do that under my parents' roof."

Living at home after college can be stifling, but it can also be liberating because it frees twentysomethings from a lot of menial, tedious responsibilities so that they can concentrate their energy and focus on other things. In this way, at the same time as it can complicate the quarterlife crisis, living at home can also ease it somewhat.

A couple of years after she graduated from Drew University (Madison, New Jersey) in 1993, Anna moved back to her parents' house in New Jersey. She returned home because she didn't have a clue where she wanted to go or what she wanted to do with her life. After two years of teaching, she had decided she actually didn't want to teach after all. She had her EMT certification, so while she was deciding what to do with her life, she earned some money by driving an ambulance. Meanwhile, living with her parents put her in a limbo in which she felt like she had regressed back into her childhood. "I had no friends when I moved back home, so I made friends with the ambulance crew— we'd go to movies. But I also hung out with my parents a lot. We're very close and it was just easier than making friends," Anna says.

While the living arrangement worked out well because she was on good terms with her family, Anna says she found herself back in the role she played as a child. "I fell back into the old style of button-pushing. I filled my role—I was always the responsible one, the one my sister called the brown-noser, the one who broke the garage door once in high school and felt awful about it for a long time," she says. "I never put up a fuss, so my parents assumed I was the same person I was before college and treated me that way. I hadn't really grown up in their eyes. I got angry with them a lot because my father would constantly give me advice—stuff like 'When you go into the bank, say you want to deposit something.'" But the time at home also gave Anna a chance to catch her breath, to step back from life as an adult and truly figure out what she wanted to do. "I learned I could never do a service-oriented job and be happy. The ambulance crew would work from nine to five, go out drinking at night, and go home, day after day," Anna says. "But if I hadn't been at home and realized that I needed more in life, I would never have moved out and gone to school."

After she graduated from college, Kristen, a 25-year-old Boulder, Colorado resident, also moved back home because she wasn't sure what to do with her life. She didn't think she would stay there very long—just temporarily, while she looked for a job. She soon discovered, however, that the ease of living at home took away some of the motivation that would have driven her to find a long-term, satisfying job. "I knew that I was capable of moving to a new city on my own. I had proven it by going to France for my master's after college, but when it came time to look into new cities in the U.S., I had a hard time figuring out where I wanted to go and what I wanted to do," she says. "In the meantime, a few job opportunities came up in the area around where my parents live, so I took them just because it was the easiest thing to do. I don't regret my decision—I found the jobs to be great experiences—but the way it worked out wasn't exactly what I had been planning on."

But the same ease of living that reduced Kristen's motivation to support herself also allowed her to figure out a new direction for her life without worrying about financial constraints. Living with her parents gave her the freedom to consider options she hadn't considered before. "During that year living with my parents, I made the decision to continue my graduate studies, and that's where I am now," she says. "Soon I will take a leave of absence for one year and move to a new city again. Part of me would like to stay here, just for the sake of continuity. This could actually be one of the reasons I stayed with my parents for a year after my master's: I wanted to be in a place with which I was familiar. I didn't want to get used to another new place. Well, next year I may be getting used to another new place. I could be going to Paris, or I could be in Belgium, an entirely new country. But I know from past experiences I'll manage wherever I go, and hopefully that year will help me figure out where my passions lie and what I'd like to do professionally."

Other twentysomethings discover that while they thought they were moving in with their parents for the financial support, they subconsciously headed home for the emotional support. Justine, a 1997 University of Utah (Salt Lake City) graduate, says that she initially moved into her parents' basement to save money, but eventually realized that the reason she stayed so long was because she treasured their encouragement. "They've been really supportive and they've encouraged me to go to graduate school, which turned out to be important to me," she says. "They understood my transition as I was graduating from college, feeling like I didn't want to come home, feeling frustrated, feeling down, and realizing that I'd spent all my life in school and now I had no choice but to jump out into the real world."

Inescapable Influence

Parents can still have an incredible influence, even on the recent graduates who doggedly live far, far away from the threat of impromptu visits and mandatory Sunday-night chicken dinners with the whole gang. Although these twentysomethings know full well that their parents are merely trying to help, the "advice" can sometimes serve only to add to the pressure.

Take Phil, a 25-year-old New Orleans native who says he was just paying his dues at a low-wage computer-help-desk job less than a year after getting an economics degree: "I was fed up with my mother calling me every week and trumpeting stories about how she read an article about some kid my age making five to six times my salary. She would say stuff like, 'There was an excellent article in *Newsweek* about Jeremy Snot-nose who's 24 years old making ninety grand programming a computerized toilet flusher at shithole.com. I'll FedEx it to you, along with some applications to graduate school that I've researched for you. . . . Oh—and the latest alumni magazine from your high school.'"

While Phil says he understands that his parents mean well, he is tired of hearing from them every time they read an article or see something on television about a person his age who is more successful than he is. Their "Why can't you do this?" attitude puts too much pressure on Phil, who says they make his life even more stressful than it already is. "I think it goes back to the old days where everyone's parents wanted them to be a doctor or marry a doctor. I'm now making more money than my mother has the entire twenty years she's been in her career, so I don't understand why she's not satisfied," he says. "This is my life and I will run it the way I want to run it. I appreciate their influence, but this is the way I'm going to live. I know that my parents don't want me to make mistakes, but this is a journey and I'm the only one who is going make decisions on this journey."

Sometimes it can be confusing for twentysomethings to decide whether the parental advice that they have relied upon for so many years is still applicable or not, as Olivia has discovered while living with her parents. "I love the romantic idea of moving out on my own to some new city, but my mother and sister have warned me that such action might result in my being very lonely. They tell me I should only move somewhere where I know someone," Olivia says. "For now, I can probably take their advice all right. I wouldn't mind going to Santa Fe or San Francisco, where I know people. But I absolutely can't obey this advice for the rest of my life. I want to travel all over the world, and perhaps live in far-off locations for a few months at a time. Shall I never go to India because I don't know anyone there? I feel this is just one of many examples of how I will be fighting my parents' advice for the rest of my life."

Liz, a 29-year-old in New York City, says that she tries to ignore her parents' advice about romantic relationships because their views are so outdated—and because they got married when they were 22 years old. "My mom gives bad advice about guys because she worries that I'll be single for a long time or won't be happy. She always tells me I'm too picky, and that I judge people too quickly," she says. "I don't think I judge as quickly as before, because I've been single for so long. If I ever find the right guy, he's got to be all these things that I want because it's my life, and if he doesn't have those things, I can't chalk it up to a character flaw. It's different now than it was when my parents got married."

And then, of course, there are the inevitable parent-inflicted guilt trips, with which most twentysomethings are intimately familiar. Just out of college, Olivia is already experiencing the inescapable pangs of guilt caused by overprotective parents. For Olivia, the thrust of the guilt is over the issue of travel, a passion of hers. Ideally, she would like to spend a few years living in various places around the world before she goes to graduate school or finds some other path to pursue. But as she is contemplating her first move, she finds her mother is already trying to rein her in. "She keeps talking about how she will miss me if I live on the other side of the country. I will miss her too, of course, but this is important to me. I think this is really the way I have to live, and I won't be happy otherwise. I want her to accept that and stop laying guilt trips on me. Does she want me to stay near home just to please her? Does she want me to resent her?" Olivia asks. "I feel I am met with parental opposition to nearly everything I want to do. They don't want me to travel alone. They don't want me to move somewhere where I don't know anyone. But to me, this is adventure, and this is the way that I must live. I don't want to be on my deathbed at age eighty-something, thinking about how I didn't do any of the things that I wanted to do. How do I reconcile my dreams and ambitions with my parents' hyperactive sense of practicality?"

The Times They Are A-Changin'

Part of the trouble here stems from the growing differences between the twentysomething generation and their parents' generation. To put it simply, times have changed, which a surprising number of today's parents have not yet acknowledged. Being a twentysomething today is a far different experience than it was when the baby boomers came of age. As Lori, a 27-year-old from Santa Fe, says, "I have difficulty with my parents because I don't think they grasp the world we live in now. It is so different in terms of jobs and opportunities. And they wonder that if we have so many opportunities, then why are we making this more difficult than it is? I think one reason my parents do this is because they did not grow up with computers and don't grasp what it means to work with them. My dad always wanted to be a doctor and my mom taught because women either went into teaching or became secretaries back then."

Phil blames the generation gap on a lack of effort on the part of the media to explain the reality of the lives of twentysomethings to the greater public. "I think there's a disconnect between people our age and older people—and it's not just a generation gap, where people don't understand us. I don't think people really understand our generation as a whole," he says. "Look at the media; they don't target anything toward us. On TV, on the news, and in the papers, nothing caters to us, and our segment is loosely defined. This affects me because I'm so concerned about where my money comes from that I can't free myself from enough of that burden to lead a lifestyle where I can just pack up and go to Colorado for a week, or travel to South America. I'm envious of that lifestyle. It's not the way most people, especially our parents, define what success is—it's more a reflection of our generation. Too many of our parents focus on the twentysomething years as all about making money and becoming a success, when this time should really be about living our lives and exploring different possibilities and potentials."

Despite the difficulties with reconciling the differences between the generations, some twentysomethings say that if they allow their parents to let go of them gradually, instead of swiftly and immediately upon graduation, then both parties will have an easier transition. "I've always believed the extent to which we rely on our parents changes on a natural basis," says Jordan, who earned a master's degree from the University of Michigan (Ann Arbor) in 1999. "As children, we depend on them for everything. During the college years, we become more reliant on ourselves and less reliant on our parents. I've never believed there was a certain point at which we shouldn't ask for help from parents. With age and maturity we notice a natural process of relying on them less."

Darryl, a 1995 graduate of the University of Montana (Missoula), suggests that twentysomethings sometimes forget that their parents have to undergo a kind of transition at this time as well. But there should be a mutual understanding that families are generally always looking out for each other's best interests. "Along the road I've moved to different cities and not accepted help from my parents," Darryl says. "In the end I learned that, one, if you move four thousand miles away your problems move with you; two, if you are fortunate enough to have parents who will help you out when you need it, don't be silly—take their help. Any parent worth a damn wants to help their kid out if they can. And three, embrace your fear. It's a good thing."

Some twentysomethings also try to remind themselves that there is one indisputable advantage to having parents who want to be involved in their twentysomething children's lives. "In the eyes of your parents you can never stop being a kid," Bert, a 24-year-old in Kansas City, Kansas, points out. "They talk to you like you're a kid and treat you like one, so why fear not being one anymore? They've been there for you through life so far (at least I hope they have), and I've found that the greatest form of flattery I can give them is to ask for their advice. I have consulted with them on every job or graduate-school decision and have learned that they are sources of great knowledge. I don't always follow their advice, because who really wants to listen to their parents? But when I sit down and swallow my pride, I find they are really very helpful (and a good source of a free meal and laundry when it gets too hectic)."

The twentysomethings who don't want to completely leave their childhoods behind just yet don't necessarily have to rely on their parents to remind them that they are still kids, though. If they have the attitude that they just don't want to grow up, some twentysomethings say, well then, they really don't have to. Matt, a 29-year-old who lives in Fairfax, Virginia, seemed shocked when we posed the question that introduces this chapter. "Stop being a kid?" he asked. "I still feel like I'm a kid." When we asked him if he'd always feel that way, he bellowed at us, *"I'm not old!"* Many twentysomethings hope that feeling never changes.

three
What If I Fail?

By the time twentysomethings in the twenty-first century graduate from college, it is highly probable that they will have heard of someone their age who has started his or her own company and made millions of dollars. Or they will have read about the latest wunderkind who has been drafted straight out of high school into a major sports league (and, again, made millions of dollars). While awareness of these kinds of successes can be frustrating, not everybody has what it takes to leap onto the Internet IPO bandwagon. And not everybody has a jump shot. But the ensuing, inescapably nagging feeling of "He did it—why haven't I?" can get pretty intense even on a smaller scale. As Bill, a 1994 graduate of Pennsylvania State University (University Park), puts it, "I have doubts when I see people that I know who are stupid and doing better than I am, when I know that I should be doing better and making more money than they are."

Maybe the slacker down the street went into thousands of dollars of credit-card debt to buy a little townhouse, rented out the rooms, and, while his friends muttered about his lack of financial responsibility, used the rent to pay off the debt and became a solid property owner. Or maybe the girl from the glee club lived out of her car and supported herself with singing gigs at seedy joints for five years before she finally hit it big with a huge record deal five years later. Most twentysomethings know about a couple of people who took enormous risks and ended up getting exactly what they wanted. Yet at the same time, despite the successes of their contemporaries (or, perhaps in some cases, because of them), many twentysomethings still just cannot convince themselves to chase after what they want, to seek out their dreams, to take risks. One of the reasons for this self-deterrence is that they cannot get past the question: "What if I fail?"

Ready, Set, Fail

The bottom line of this chapter (for anyone who doesn't particularly feel like reading any further) might very well be that people fail and live to tell about it, though that concept does not stop twentysomethings from fretting about the idea of failure. Tom, a 1994 graduate of Rutgers University (New Brunswick, New Jersey), says that, like most people, he is afraid to fail. But he has failed before and survived, so he knows that if he fails again, he will still be all right. If friends had told him the day he graduated that five years later he would be where he is now, he would have laughed at them. He was a good student in high school and college, where life was easy for him despite his rigorous academic and music schedules. He left college as a self-assured graduate with a commission in the United States Navy's rigorous nuclear power program, the only naval program that requires both an interview and an oral exam during the admissions process. Then he began the training. "I had struggled through the nuclear power program, a rigorous training pipeline that prepares young officers and enlisted men and women to operate the nuclear reactors that power some of the world's greatest naval vessels. After reporting to my first boat, a submarine, I began the qualification process that would prove to be my most difficult undertaking yet. After almost a year on board, and several failed attempts at completing an oral board for my watch station, I was called into the captain's stateroom and told that I was being transferred off the boat, in the best interests of both myself and the boat. I was devastated. Here was a man—my boss—who was essentially telling me that I could no longer do my job, the job I had been trained to do since the first day I was in the service. The word failure was the only one that came to mind," Tom says. "As I staggered back to my bunk to collect my belongings, holding back the tears that inevitably come with learning you have failed, the navigator, one of my mentors on the boat, pulled me into his stateroom and told me I had failed. 'So what,' were his next words. 'This is the first time in your life that you have not accomplished something you set out to do, I would guess,' he continued. 'But the true measure of you as a person, the true measure of success, will be how you deal with it and move on.'"

Easier said than done, Tom thought. The Navy relocated him to a remote duty station where he would serve out the remaining time left on his commitment until he could assimilate into civilian life. But rather than dwell on a failure that overturned everything he had set out to do in his life, he used his downfall to renew his determination. "That last tour of mine became my last chance to succeed in the Navy. So rather than sit back and let the time pass me by, I took every opportunity afforded me to succeed, and I made opportunity where there was none. I left my mark on that base, as I had in high school, as I had in college. It was that tour that gives me the positive outlook I have toward the Navy, instead of the bitter hatred I might have felt if I had let my first failure become a part of me," he says. "Without a doubt, yes

I am still afraid of failing. But in accordance with old clichés, I am a better person for it. I certainly will fail again. I set my goals and aspirations high enough that there is bound to be a time when I will not reach them. But that's the only way I know how to do things. And it is not in my failure that I define myself, but in my ability to move beyond it and make something of myself with what's left."

When we did the interviews for this book, we did not set out to end up with a bunch of Aesop's fables. We weren't particularly interested in illustrating any life lessons, just as we knew that twentysomethings weren't particularly interested in reading them. Spewing clichés is boring. (Besides, that's what parents are for.) We just wanted to tell it like it is. But Tom was not the only recent graduate who emerged from his failure with an optimistic attitude. Part of the quarterlife crisis involves dreading the idea of failure in some aspect of life. But one of the ways to muddle through the crisis, it seems, is the act of failing in the first place.

After graduating from Barnard College (New York City) in 1997, Nora moved to Israel, where she wanted to incorporate art into her professional life. "I was on an optimistic high, feeling as though I could do anything and everything," she says. "I sent my résumé to all of the museums, and contacted anyone people referred me to. Finally I got a reply. I had an interview at a tiny museum for the position of tour guide in a former artist's home. This was my foot in the door, my big chance. I remember how intimidated I was at the mere thought of meeting the curator. During my interview I enthusiastically tried to convince her that I was the perfect person for the job. I guess my broken Hebrew did not sell her on the idea of me being her future employee. She requested that I prepare for a week and then return to give her a mock tour. Although I am a pretty outgoing person and I am confident in public speaking, I knew that my Hebrew was my big disadvantage. For a week I researched the artist and his works. I came up with a tour that was filled with creative ideas, in the hope that my effort, creativity, and knowledge would get me the position. The night before the mock guide, I gave my tour to a group of friends. My Hebrew level was so poor that they told me to ask for an extension, so that I could prepare a memorized speech written with their help. That is what I did. When the day arrived, I knew my speech like the back of my hand, but the words weren't mine, and half of what I was saying was in a vocabulary obviously not my own. Needless to say, I was completely humiliated. I forgot half my speech, and every room we moved to another person came along to listen with a look of pity. I did not get the position."

For the next two months, Nora moped. She considered leaving both Israel and the art world as she sulked about her humiliation. "Then one day, a friend of mine told me that if I didn't see myself as an Israeli, nobody else would. Something inside of me clicked," she says. "I began to speak only Hebrew, and with time my confidence increased. Months later I got an interview at the Israel Museum in Jerusalem, where the woman interviewing me told me that after talking to me for two minutes, she knew I was perfect for the job. Currently I am studying toward a master's in art history (in Hebrew), working at a gallery in Jaffa (in Hebrew), and working at the Israel Museum (in Hebrew and English). Now I have more art in my life than I ever imagined. I did it."

Nora did it, but a lot of twentysomethings don't. One enormous realm of failure is the technology sector, where the big, quick rewards are legendary. Scores of twentysomethings salivate over the idea of taking their own Internet company public or selling it for scads of stock options. These days, recent graduates hear about their peers accomplishing these feats all of the time. What they hear about much less frequently is that a greater number of their peers are failing. Bert, a 24-year-old who lives in Kansas City, Kansas, formed an Internet start-up with dreams of taking it public within three years. "I had the highest hopes of hitting it big when I left my job to start a 'dot com' business. It was a great time, but when the savings were gone one year later, I had great experience, good stories, and increased job marketability, but no functioning business. I was in credit card debt up the wazoo, and guess what? I had to move in with my parents for five months so that I could get out of debt," he says. But while he wishes he hadn't failed, Bert hardly regrets the experience. Partly because he had failed at something, learned from it, and then managed to put it behind him, he was accepted into a top-tier business school. "Even failures, at this age, can be successes. We will all fail, but that is what life is about—learning from our mistakes," he says. "You have to give up that chance to fail when you get married or when you have kids, because others are relying on you. Right now, though, life is free and yours to screw up as you please."

"The time is now"—a thought that many twentysomethings echo—is one reason that the twenties are so difficult. "The time is now" means there is a pressure to achieve now, to dream now, and to resolve things now, because there will be less of an opportunity to do so later. "When do you give up your dreams? Not now. I'm 25," says Rick, who lives in New York City. "When do you pack them in? Tough one. When a risk for a dream might hurt your kids, wife, or family. But definitely not now."

Going After the Dream

Some twentysomethings say that, as Bert and Rick suggest, fellow recent graduates need to realize that because in their twenties they are usually accountable only to themselves, this is the best time in their lives to fail. As a result, these optimists paradoxically keep a positive attitude precisely by expecting failure. If they expect to fail, they reason, then any good that comes out of a situation is a pleasant surprise. "Of course

I'm going to fail. A little bit. That's what this period of time is all about. We're supposed to fail. We're supposed to build character. We're supposed to not know what we're doing a hundred percent of the time. I think that the problem with the idea of growing up is that we trade our sense of adventure for this notion of stability," says Brandon, a 24-year-old who lives in Los Angeles. "Me, I want to write for sitcoms. I have absolutely no idea how long it is going to take to get me there. I do know that I wouldn't be satisfied with myself if I didn't try to do something I'm passionate about. Living in a world where 'What if' is the game I play to save my sanity because I hate the rest of my life is what I would consider real failure. Counting the days on my job until retirement comes along is what I would consider real failure."

Brandon is currently pursuing his dream of becoming a sitcom writer by using every method he possibly can. He has gotten a foot in a door, sent out letters, networked, applied for fellowships, and met the right people. But he is still trying, and he wonders how long it will take. "This leads into the next question: knowing when to say when. The sheer notion of having to give up my dreams is painful," he says. "I don't know if you can put an actual time limit on this, but I think it has to do with your overall state of mind. It's like being a 35-year-old Triple-A baseball player. Lots of people must look at those guys and think, 'Okay, Tubbo, time to find a real job and give up your pipe dream of playing in the big leagues.' Maybe he does. But then again, maybe in continuing after his dreams, he finds his real passion is in molding the kids fresh out of high school and he becomes a coach. Or a scout. Or a teacher. There's no rule that says you have to like your job just as much in year five as you did in year one. From the professionals that I've talked to, I think the ones that are the most satisfied are the ones who have held tight to the idea that it's okay to be mobile, to try new things, to leave that cushy desk job for something more scary but utterly more fulfilling."

Brandon says that a good analogy for his outlook on failure is dating, because dating involves rejection, and rejection is a form of failure. "Asking a girl out can be an absolutely terrifying experience," he says. "Why? What's the worst that can happen? She says no and you move on. Well, sometimes that's true, but sometimes, as George McFly said, 'I just don't know if I can take that kind of rejection.' Inevitably, you wake up the next day and you're still the same guy, you still have the same friends, none of whom like you any less because some stupid chick told you to make like a tree and get outta here. And then you think to yourself, you know what? It's her loss. I'm a great guy. I'm going places. And I'll find another girl, even cooler and better-looking, and she'll say, 'Yes I will go out on a date with you.' . . . Of course, you're much better prepared the next time around. And by better prepared, I mean that the next time you're faced with a similar situation, you will make sure that she has been drinking heavily before you ask her any questions. (Okay, at this point, I think the analogy stops working as well. Unfortunately, in coming up with this analogy, I've come to the realization that practically every woman I've been with since I went to college has been in some state of inebriation beforehand.)"

Fermented grains aside, Sandra, a 25-year-old from Birmingham, Alabama, is in the midst of acting on this "What's the worst that can happen?" philosophy. Sandra says she knew she had to ditch her technology career in favor of trying to become an interior decorator when one day she pondered what she would do if she had the security to do whatever she wanted with her life. "Recently, I decided to take the plunge. It was this huge flash of light, like a message in the sky," she says. "I had a cold, and I was totally stressed because I was trying to look for a new job in computers, and I went home to take a quick nap. When I woke up, the thought that was in my head was that if I were independently wealthy, I would sit around and decorate houses all the time. And that's when it hit me that decorating is actually a career. I just knew that was my passion. I'm just now having a dream for the first time in my life, so I'm not about to give it up now."

But just because she is steadfastly focused on her dream does not mean Sandra isn't afraid of failing. As she points out, along with the joy of pursuing a dream comes the fear—that gnawing 'What if' in the pit of the stomach—that it might not work out. And if it doesn't work out, it can have a domino effect on other aspects of a twentysomething's life. "I'm really worried about failure," Sandra says. "I'm worried that I won't make very much money as a decorator. You pretty much don't make money until you own your own business, and I won't be able to afford to start my own business for a while. You also need a master's degree, and the best college that offers that degree will cost me more than $30,000. That's lots and lots and lots of money, and I'm so scared that I'll fail, that I'll end up in debt. I'm also all torn up because I live alone, which is really expensive in this area. So I'm stressed about that. I keep wondering if I'm really doing the right thing."

As Sandra indicates, failure at one thing can start off a chain reaction of failures in other aspects of life. This can cause extreme stress for twentysomethings because they don't necessarily have one settled rock of stability—marriage, property, career—that will always be there no matter what happens. But if Sandra doesn't at least try, she says, she will never know if her dream could work, which is why she is taking the risk.

Abort Mission

One possible way for twentysomethings to try to dodge failure at every turn is to change their dreams as they go along—not to compromise them, but just to realize that as they themselves change, so might their dreams. This is not necessarily a bad thing. As Tracy, a 1994 Princeton University (New Jersey) graduate, says, "When do I give up my dreams? I hope I never give up on them, but I do think they change as I change."

Mark, a 29-year-old in New York City, decided to change his dream rather than accept failure. An overachiever who excelled at several things, he discovered during college that he was a good enough actor to try to make a living out of it. After graduation, he bicycled across the country with a friend to clear his head, and then dove into the New York City acting scene. As a struggling actor for the next four years, Mark met artists, dancers, and musicians who encouraged his acting. He sang in a band for a few months, joined a few theater companies, and performed in several off-Broadway productions. But he didn't make it. "Here's my take on my mind-set at the time: When I came out of college, I was hungry. Hungry for success, hungry for recognition, and hungry to make my mark," he says. "But I was unfocused and didn't have a good overall plan. My eagerness as a 22-year-old was stymied by my lack of knowledge of how the world works. Twenty-two-year-olds are arrogant, cocky, beautiful, and feel like they can do anything. That's how I felt, but after a few years in New York City, I realized that the theater world in New York is a tough place to make a living. If I had gone straight to Los Angeles after college, I bet I would have been cast on a soap opera or something similar. Not that that necessarily would have been better, but it would have been a smarter move for me as an actor. Of course, I didn't realize this at the time." When Mark eventually did go to Los Angeles, he lost his taste for "the nasty business that is acting." But he had come this far, and he didn't want to have to view the past four years as a waste. So he took some screenwriting and film-making classes at UCLA and wrote three screenplays. His new dream, he says, is to direct.

Often, for various reasons, dreams don't work out, whether, like Tom, a twentysomething just isn't good enough, or whether, like Nora, more experience is necessary. One of the questions twentysomethings face while contemplating the pursuit of their dreams is when to go for it and when to give up. Recent graduates can have a tough time deciding when to admit failure and move on, or when to just put dreams aside for a little while so they can try again at a more conducive moment. They also have a tough time deciding whom to blame.

Penny, a 1999 graduate of Syracuse University (New York), insists that she clings to her dreams with a defiant zeal as a way of striking back at the adults who mold the "real world" into a convention that suppresses dreaming. "I don't want to give up my dreams, and I never will. How cliché and *Breakfast Club*–sounding, but it's true. I want my soul, thank you, and right now I've got more than James Brown," she says. "I am still human, though, and after initially quitting my job for my dream, I realized both just what was so precious about it and what I would kiss good-bye with delight. It is amazing how much I have actually been thrown into this 'real world' thing. I believe the 'real world' expression was created by middle-aged adults who wanted to give credibility and a concrete environment to the disaster they created for themselves. Not to say that I won't fall into the same trap. But these are the dreams we speak of. In the real world they only exist in a repressed form. It seems people keep suppressing themselves in this fictional place to make up for the sheer fact that they are afraid of failing."

However she rails against the way the traditionally practical idea of the "real world" stifles the passions of idealistic youths, Penny does admit that she put her own dreams aside because of her fear of failure. Essentially, she says she sold out: she ditched her job and planned to leave her city in order to pursue a career in holistic health, and then took a corporate job in the very city she said she would abandon. "I am definitely afraid of failing, and I never cease to be amazed by how my subconscious continually sabotages my actions via this fear. I am trying to fight it, but now I am amidst this confusion of my job and identity and my ethics, rather than a path. So how did this happen? I have been asking myself this for the past few days. My excuse to myself is résumé padding. But it's an interesting job that I'm hoping to combine with a degree in alternative medicine to do consulting. I'm hoping I don't buy into the corporate b.s., but I have to learn to live in a capitalistic society. That is what is here. If I were you, I'd think that I'm trying to convince myself as I am saying this," she says. "I know you asked for answers, but isn't this all about the questions we have? Isn't that the quintessential element of this period—questioning? It just varies by degree from person to person. I just want to fulfill my dream now, and something is holding me back. I wish I knew whether it was intuition or fear. Probably both. So I will read about my passion, save my money, and make it a reality eventually. I just hope I get that chance. I just resigned, and on my computer radio is 'Angel from Montgomery,' and suddenly the lines 'How the hell can a person go to work in the morning, come home in the evening, and have nothing to say?' have a much more profound meaning."

Feeling forced to buy into conventional notions of practicality is one reason twentysomethings postpone their dreams, but a bigger reason is money—which is one of the top motivators for recent graduates both to pursue a dream and to give one up. Kim, a 25-year-old from Augusta, Georgia, has changed jobs three times in three years while pursuing her dream of being a financially solvent preschool teacher. "I gave up my dreams for greater financial stability and regained them at the cost of relationships and time," she says. "I discovered a passion and aptitude for teaching preschool children. I believe it to be the single most fascinating, emotionally rewarding, intellectually stimulating, and worthwhile profession there is. Unfortunately, the financial rewards are roughly on par with that of a retail worker. This sucks. I spent my childhood and early adolescence loudly proclaiming money is irrelevant to me as long as I love my job, respect myself and my career, and am fundamentally happy. I still believe that to be true except that the last bit is a tremendous difficulty. I discovered, once I was forced to pay my own bills (often late) and eat food that I had to buy (often tasting like and containing the dietary equivalent of, roughly, dirty gym socks), that being happy on a preschool teacher's salary was nigh onto impossible. In fact, initially I was earning approximately $4,000 less than my college cost per year. This was unacceptable. As a result, I abandoned my love of teaching for the greater economic rewards of being a nanny."

Kim found a family that both intellectually stimulated her and made her feel as if she was using the skills and knowledge she had honed during her training to become a preschool teacher. The family had recently adopted two Russian children who had emotional problems and no grasp of the English language. Kim flourished. "They are brilliant, vibrant, wonderful, energetic, emotional, defiant, and difficult children. Happily, those traits rank among my favorites in people, particularly those under four feet tall," she says. "I enjoyed working with the family tremendously, though I found the emotional roller coaster both unnerving and exhausting." But, like Penny, she says that someday she will pursue her dream again.

Plan B

Rather than wait to see if they fail, and then scramble to recover if they do, many twentysomethings start two courses of action simultaneously so that they have a backup option in case they need it. Fallback plans are also essential because, as Natasha, a 1996 graduate of Prince George's Community College (Largo, Maryland) says, "If you get what you dream of, you may end up at a loss, because what do you dream of after that? And what if your dream isn't what you anticipated? Life always has a way of presenting options that will make you happy, so it's best to learn to roll with the punches. The day you do give up on your dream is a sad one, but make sure there's another, more realistic one to take its place."

When Natasha graduated from college with a degree in music, she desperately wanted to be an opera singer, but, she says, "that was just not realistic (although it could still happen). I haven't given up on it, but I also knew that my stagnant dream sure wasn't paying the rent." So she strung together several artsy-type jobs in order to be able to pay her bills. She interned in the media relations department of a performing-arts center and worked part-time at a publishing company for two years. Then she did administrative work for a wine organization. "My need was to be creative, so I lasted five months before I quit," she says. "By chance I was hired at an Internet technology company where I am learning HTML and enhancing my graphic skills. So I'm doing something I enjoy more, but now I'm feeling confined by corporate America. I don't know if I'll ever find something where I don't get bored occasionally or want to change after five months. But at least I'm making money. A few people in the world have jobs they love. I am not one of those people. But I'm happy and my job is working as a stepping stone to help me realize what will eventually have to be a new dream, even though I don't know what that dream is yet."

Tara, a 1994 graduate of Clark University (Worcester, Massachusetts), suggests that backup plans are sometimes necessary to help twentysomethings move on with their lives. But that doesn't make them easy. Tara decided she didn't have what it took to be a dancer. Now, after going back to school for a master's in public health, she is reluctantly trying to reenter the working world on her backup plan. "Now that I'm moving out of the academic world and will no longer survive by wit and charm alone (ha ha), I'm terrified. I try to tell myself that I know what I'll need to do. I know my strengths and weaknesses and will hopefully remember what to focus on in school and beyond. But I'm still terrified," she says. "Entry into the working world and entry into the cerebral world, as opposed to the sensory, physical world of the arts, is quite a culture shock. So, I tell myself, the fear and self-doubt will pass as I grow more accustomed to this role. I tell myself."

Sometimes, in the process of coming up with a back-up plan, twenty-somethings are so unimpressed with the alternatives that they motivate themselves further to succeed at a top-choice career instead. This happened to Emily, a 22-year-old living in Los Angeles, who started thinking about fallback options when she realized that until she achieves her dream of becoming a screenwriter, she is not entirely sure what to tell people that she actually does for a living. She says, "The question 'What if I fail?' is very familiar to me because I'm a screenwriter. Or trying to be a screenwriter. I mean, I want to be a screenwriter, and I was training to be a screenwriter, so I guess that makes me now kind of sort of a screenwriter—albeit unemployed. Since graduation, people have asked me several times about my occupation. I make my living by working for an educational services company, though I feel that this is just temporary until my screenwriting career picks up. So in response do I tell people I'm a writer? Or a wannabe writer? Or an unemployed writer? Or a tutor? I usually hesitate, bite my lip, and give a very weak 'I'm trying to be a screenwriter. . . . It's slow, you know, but we'll see, it's a hard business,' and then I babble until the person nods politely and continues with the conversation. When I have a setback, when people don't like my work, or like it but still don't buy it, and don't hire me, I think to myself, what if I fail? What will I do? My training is very limited to precisely this: screenwriting. I can't write newspaper columns, or books, or perhaps even advertisement copy. I don't have credentials to teach or fix cars or whatever other jobs people in this country have. Honestly, I'm not even really that clear on what other professions there are. I am so unfamiliar with the idea of not being a screenwriter that failing becomes like *the nothing*. My entire life I've only wanted this, so I really have no idea how to handle a negative outcome."

The prospect of failing was petrifying to Emily because she had no idea what else she would do with her life. She came up with some other options, just in case, so that if she ever reaches a moment when she knows she has to give up her dream, she won't be entirely at a loss. But when she managed to come up with vaguely acceptable backup options, she only became more determined not to have to fall back on them. "One day I actually started to plan for such a debacle. It was a low day—my friends seemed to be leaping ahead while I was having trouble writing a line of dialogue and several pages were in desperate need of repair," she says. "So I said fine, I guess it's time I figure out my Plan B. I could go back to school and be a teacher (mental image: me in a tweed jacket with patches on the elbows, solemnly smoking a pipe while I seethe about the film industry that rejected me); I could be an office temp for life (mental image: me returning home in my worn peach suit to my shabby apartment filled with nothing but beanie babies, my only solace); I could marry for money (mental image: me driving an SUV through a picket fence—car seats, and diaper bags a jumble). I kept being distracted by other images, those having to do with what I really want. I want to write and I want someone to pay me for it. I want to see my characters and my stories on the screen; I want other people to enjoy them, and discuss them, and be overjoyed and enraged by them. I want this so badly it hurts and when I picture this life that I want, I am suddenly at peace and I suddenly see that there is no other way. I could say that I cannot fail because I am not trained to do anything else, but I really think the truth is that I cannot fail because I simply won't give up. I could be 40 and still trying, but I'll still be in the game, on my way, on the verge, which might be close enough. But even that scenario is unacceptable, so I continue planning my life by the next few months, and then the next few years. I still have Plans B, C, D, E, and F, but these are not plans of how I'll live if Plan A of writing falls through. Instead, they are plans of how to get back to Plan A and keep my dream."

Methods of avoiding or combating the prospect of failure vary by the individual, but there are a few outlooks that many recent graduates share. One perspective is that, as Emily suggests, if a twentysomething simply never gives up, then he or she will never have to admit to failure. "Never give up your dreams," offers Robin, a 23-year-old from Lincoln, Nebraska. "Why do something that won't bring about your dreams? Life is short enough—don't waste it working in a job that doesn't drive you. It might take a dizzyingly intricate path to lead to those dreams, but at least the end result is what you have striven for. I want to look back on my life years from now and say, 'I was not working at my job; I was having fun doing something I enjoy while getting paid for it.' That way I know that I have lived my life to its fullest extent."

Another perspective is that twentysomethings should just go with the flow. It seems simple, but it works for the people who can live their lives that way. Taylor, a 26-year-old from Orlando, Florida, says nobody can figure out how he managed to get a job at one of the top Internet companies in the country, but once he did, he just went with it. "I didn't pay much attention to anything, particularly. I had a job offer; I did the job. I don't consider it a career—it's just a job. I didn't really consider not failing or anything; I just figured I'd take it one day at a time," he says. "I don't believe in deferred enjoyment. I believe in enjoying myself right now, so that's how I live my life—job, everything. There's not a lot of mystery to it. It's very straightforward. So whether I'm doing this job or something else, I'm enjoying my life. That's all there is to it. People complicate it themselves. No point in worrying about things that haven't happened yet. Instead, concentrate on what's happening right now and your future will be successful. Nothing's permanent, nothing's forever. That's one thing I've learned. So if you're having fun now, it's fine. I don't particularly worry about it because I'm buoyant. I'll float in one direction or another. I've ended up where I'm supposed to be, so I figure it will continue that way."

Twenty-nine year-old Derrick also suggests that the secret to putting aside fear of failure is to try not to worry about the "What ifs," although this positive outlook might be due to the nature of Derrick's own dream—he has tried for years to be a comedy writer in Hollywood. "Yes, you are going to fail and wind up penniless in the gutter, covered in festering wounds with nothing but a stray dog to keep you company. Seriously, though: maybe you will fail; hopefully you won't. There's no way to tell. But, the more time you spend dwelling on the possibility of your failure, the less time you'll spend concentrating on the task at hand, thus increasing the likelihood of failure. So don't worry about failure. It will happen on its own. A wise man once said, 'Don't look back. They might be gaining on you.' Never give up your dreams. If you're lucky enough to actually have one, then you owe it to yourself to hang onto it. How do you know if you should chase your dreams in the first place? Ask yourself two questions. One, is there anything else besides this I can see myself doing? Because you will hit that point before you make it in your chosen field. For example, you really want to race Formula One cars, but you could also see yourself as a dental hygienist. You will probably reach that point where you seriously consider becoming a dental hygienist. So, sometimes it helps if you have *no* alternatives. The second thing you need to ask yourself is, 'Am I good enough?' Say you really, really, *really* want to be a fashion model. But you've got a face only a mother could love, and a huge ass. You need to understand that your chances of making a living as a super-model are very slim. Another (more realistic) example: You want to be a novelist. Are you a good writer? Have people (teachers, friends) always told you that you have a way with the written word? If so, you might have a shot. If you've gotten nothing but D's in English, a 350 on the SAT verbal, and nobody's ever said anything encouraging to you about your writing, think about it before you take the plunge. The more difficult your chosen endeavor, the more it helps to have some kind of natural ability."

It's worth considering this outlook. After seven years of operating under this philosophy, Derrick nailed his ultimate goal—he just sold a screenplay to a major motion picture company in Hollywood. The possibility of failure, it seems, is just a matter of perspective.

four
What Do All of These Doubts Mean?

I n the Introduction, we talked about how the quarterlife crisis can become hazardous because it can cause depression. We also mentioned that the most difficult part of the quarterlife crisis could be the multitude of doubts that often seem to hit a twentysomething all at once. Suddenly, for all of the reasons that twentysomethings discuss in this book—identity problems, anxiety at becoming an adult, fear of failure, inexperience with making major decisions, trouble balancing their lives, and a feeling that college didn't prepare them for much of anything—the world is new, and frightening, and hard, and unrelenting, and not at all what they had expected. They question themselves and their ability to handle these new challenges. And sometimes these doubts turn dangerous.

What can compound this intense feeling of self-doubt is that, because twentysomethings generally don't discuss these extremely personal misgivings, they don't know that other people their age are going through exactly the same thing. As a result, they feel that their problems—sadness, melancholy, panic, anger, apathy—are abnormal, which makes them doubt themselves even more. "I felt like something was wrong with me," says Kelly, a 27-year-old in Reno, Nevada. "It seemed like all of the other people who had recently graduated from college were excited to finally be on their own and ready to be adults, just like that. They were going out, having fun, making money, getting their own places, and meeting new people, as if everything was just a smooth ride from here on out. But there I was, scared out of my mind. I would think about my peers, all happy, carefree, and mellow, and I would just curl up and cry because I felt like I was the only person who was finding this time of life so damn hard. I wish I had said something to my friends back then. I wish I had known then that a lot of that seemingly carefree attitude was just a front—that they were as scared as I was, but hiding it differently."

The proliferation of doubts, which seemed to keep multiplying as she tried to take on the responsibilities of being an adult, were constantly on Kelly's mind. She would try to let go of them, but then she would think of something else to question, and they would start all over again. "It was this whirling downward spiral, a rapidly increasing cycle, like a concentric circle that kept expanding and suffocating all of my other thoughts. There was just no room for anything else to think about. I kept asking myself things like, 'What will I do with my life?' 'Can I ever be happy at a job or will it always be just work?' 'Is all of adulthood this stifling and monotonous?' 'Will I ever be sure enough about somebody to marry him if I can't even be sure about myself?' 'Am I going to feel this hopeless for the rest of my life?' 'Why is everyone else handling this more easily than I am?' and there were more and more of these questions that I just couldn't get around. I gave myself headaches because I was worrying about this relentlessly. I withdrew from my friends and incessantly snapped at my boyfriend, who tried to understand what I was going through. Eventually, eight months after I graduated, I just broke down," she says. One day at work, when Kelly realized, yet again, that she was already counting down the number of hours in the day and it was only ten o'clock in the morning, she panicked. "I just felt so helpless—I couldn't catch my breath, my heart was racing, and I just felt so overwhelmed by this heavy cloud of sadness hanging over me. I left work for the day and immediately went to my doctor, who gave me the full battery of tests. When she told me she thought I had fallen into a depression, I thought, 'That couldn't be me. I was never like that.' And then I realized that that's what this transition had turned me into—this sad, antisocial person whom I myself didn't even like. And I felt more alone than ever."

Kelly says she was put on antidepressants for a few months, which dulled her melancholy and freed up some of her brainpower to think about things other than her intense self doubts. "Depression is hard, and it is strange, and it makes you question who you really are. And sometimes you lose yourself within the person you become when you're depressed. The antidepressants stopped the headaches and freed me from the urgent sense of panic I felt whenever I tried to think about my future. It was hard to distinguish moods because I couldn't tell if I was really content with something or if it was only the antidepressants talking, although they did allow me to catch my breath. But they didn't 'cure' anything. Despite the daily pills, I was still very scared of the idea of adulthood hitting me so quickly," she says. "It's funny, the thing that finally got me out of that seemingly interminable haze. Here I was, sobbing every other day, frantic with worry about how I was going to make this transition that I wasn't ready for, withdrawing from the world, doubting myself into a frenzy, and actively snubbing people who tried to help, when it turned out that the only thing I really needed to hear—the one thing that freed me to become myself again—was that it was completely normal for twentysomethings to go through this period of helplessness."

Kelly's experience was hardly abnormal, but because she had never heard her friends—or the media, or onscreen twentysomething characters—talk about it, she was afraid that something was terribly wrong with her. Other twentysomethings say that the transition hit them just as intensely. "I struggled with horrific self-esteem problems," says Kim, a 25-year-old in Augusta, Georgia. "I developed a pseudo-person to exhibit to the outside universe and pushed my true self so far down that I didn't even know I was playacting. Though I was bright, funny, warm, and well liked, I despised myself with an intensity that continues to shock and distress me."

This chapter, frankly, is not an upper. Dozens of twentysomethings told us their stories of hardship, of bouts with depression and feelings of panic. They are staggeringly honest about these very personal matters. We share them with you here because many of them told us that if they had only known how common it is to get depressed because of this transition, they might not have gotten depressed in the first place.

Doubts and Questions

Both a cause and a symptom of the kind of depression that young adults feel after they leave college is the prevalence of doubts. While everyone experiences some form of doubts throughout their lives, twentysomethings—who are often trying to arrange all facets of their lives at the same time—can experience doubts about everything, all at once, says Jason, a 1996 graduate of the University of Chicago. "It gets darkest before dawn. The doubts come in clumps: How am I going to get a new job, a new apartment, and, in my earlier twenties, how am I going to find someone to spend my life with? I had doubts about all of these things, plus I'm a teacher, which isn't always a respectable position in terms of money and status, so I have doubts about that," he says. "The doubts have the tendency to make you feel depressed about your life. A lot of my friends have needed to see therapists because of this, but they haven't gone because there's a stigma and because a lot of my friends are male, which makes it harder to admit to another male that you need help. Plus it's expensive and a lot of them are unemployed. The reason we all have these problems at this particular point in life is because of the sudden change from college. When you go away to college, you at least have that backdrop as a structure for your life. You have a purpose, which is to go to class and get an education. And then you graduate and you have to form your own structure. For twenty-two years in one form or another, you're fully accountable to a set of rules. You're going to school, and then, all of a sudden, you're not. You have to form your own social circles. You have to carve your own niche out wherever you settle, and there's no guidebook for that. So you don't know what to do, and you doubt yourself over and over again, and then sometimes you fall into a depression."

Amy, a 26-year-old from Philadelphia, says that she constantly undergoes a barrage of intensive interrogation periods—from herself. She thinks that she is hit with all of these questions now because she is wrestling between what she wants and what she realistically knows she can get. "I've been out of college now for four years," she says. "I've been working ever since I graduated, and I started having serious doubts about my future career interests early during my second year. I think I struggle with wanting everything. I want to pursue my personal fantasies, desires, interests. At the same time I want the guarantee of financial stability that my consulting job will certainly provide for me. I'm a basket case with all of the troubling questions that infest my mind. I really believe that it's an unusual period in any person's life. To be twentysomething, wanting everything in life, wanting the financial security of the job but not ready to push aside personal dreams, desires, and fantasies. As a twentysomething, it's difficult to find contentment. You're just out of college, it's your first or second job, and you're searching for personal contentment in your life. Often times this means an assessment of what the hell it is you're doing for most of the day. Is this what I want to do for the rest of my life? It's a question that still infests my mind day in and day out. I sometimes visualize my twentysomething identity crisis as a wedding ceremony. I'm walking down the aisle and I see the man I'm about to marry, and I think to myself, 'Wow, is this the person that I will spend the rest of my life with?'"

Twentysomethings have a tendency to try to avoid confronting these types of issues, which only makes it more difficult when they are eventually forced to deal with them, Amy suggests. Denial, as they say, ain't just a river in Egypt. "What do we do? We want change because we believe that change in all things is good (Socrates). We believe change will resolve some of the fears we have because it wipes the slate clean—a change of scenery, a new set of coworkers to substitute for the ones you hated. Come on. The majority of the time, it's an excuse to avoid reality. In the long run, you're just walking down another path that cycles back to the inevitable: What the hell am I doing with my life? So now comes the stage where you get quite bored. You think you're getting older, so you stop and think, 'Oh crap. Why am I doing this? Why didn't I climb Mount Everest, join the Peace Corps, save the rain forests? Why didn't I get that Ph.D. in ancient Greek philosophy? Why didn't I do something that really makes a difference, helps starving children in third world countries, or find a cure for the AIDS epidemic?' This (at 25) might be the last opportunity for me to do something completely outrageous, exciting, and unconventional, instead of following the traditional route of a consulting job for a few years and then business school. That would be the most logical and sensible path for me. Instead, I'm stuck in a desk job, providing assistance to clients who already know what they want, but want me to hold their hand, console them, and make them pay my company outrageous billing rates for me to regurgitate what they already know, but in consultant lingo. We are extremely disillusioned individuals who are intimidated by making changes, taking risks. I mean, how can we throw away financial security and career opportunities to do something creative, interesting, inspiring—to throw caution to the wind and join the Peace Corps? What would our friends, families, colleagues say? What if I make the wrong choice and have lost out on success, respect, and money by leaving it all behind? How will I get back into step with the level of success and financial viability of my friends who stuck with it?"

Working Problems

It doesn't always take a flood of questions or doubts to unleash a depression in a twentysomething. Sometimes it is enough if one aspect of life doesn't turn out well, presents unexpected difficulties, or diminishes self-esteem to the point that it creates one huge doubt that controls a twentysomething's emotions. One of the most common impetuses for this effect is work—both trying to find it and then coping with it. This is what Joanna, who earned a master's degree from Bucknell University (Lewisburg, Pennsylvania) in 2000, says led her into a depression. "College doesn't prepare you for the real world emotionally, which definitely brought on a depression for me," she says. "Going to a therapist helped, but it was really more about coming to the realization that this is what the real world is like. The difference from college that I encountered in my first job was this environment that was sterile, not nurturing, and full of people who didn't care about my welfare or happiness or well-being, partly because it might be in their best interest to 'do better' than me. At the same time that I found myself walking into a den of hostility day after day, I also realized that the bottom had dropped out of my social world."

The striking difference between the sheltered school setting and the cold atmosphere at work left Joanna feeling miserable as she wondered if this was what adult life was supposed to be like. "Mostly I remember two phases of life and corresponding frames of mind: the 'work' phase, which basically involved hating the moment I had to open my eyes and go to work, and which began to let up only about an hour before I could go home; and the 'after-work' phase, which involved filling up hours with basically brainless activities so I wouldn't have to think about going to work the next day," she says. "It wasn't that hating work just ruined my work week; it also ruined my weekends. It pervaded my whole life. When I look back on the three years I spent working after college, it seems to me I did an awful lot of TV watching. I've been an avid reader my whole life, but somehow TV just seemed a lot easier. It allowed me to turn off my mind for a while and totally escape. I started to find novels depressing, even though I never had before. In the evenings I went out because I felt like I had to, but not because I wanted to. And by Sundays the foreboding sense of Monday was always upon me and it seemed to rob the day of any pleasure. I remember always thinking, 'It's Sunday, I've got to enjoy myself!'—an imperative, rather than something you would just do. And usually I'd sit around and watch TV and end up feeling guilty about it."

After she had been in the working world for a while, Joanna was in such bad shape that she started taking antidepressants. "I was missing work because of stress-related problems—bad stomachaches, throwing up, migraine headaches. The worst part was realizing that no one at work was interested in changing the source of my problems there—the work being incredibly boring and unstimulating, and also requiring staying for extra hours after work without being compensated. I would try to talk to my boss about how the job could be changed not only to my advantage but to the advantage of the whole workplace, how it could be more efficient and less tedious. He seemed sympathetic and agreed to talk to his boss about it; a week later I was told my contract wouldn't be renewed at the end of a year and I'd have to find a new job," she says. "That's when I realized that all the things college provided for you, like academic advisors and RAs and professional therapists if you needed someone to talk to—these safety nets had no equivalent in real life. And by trying to talk out my problems, by trying to change the parameters of my job to everyone's advantage, I sabotaged myself in a way that was obviously detrimental as far as being unemployed, but also incredibly painful. The sense of rejection and humiliation over being fired would have been bad enough, but to have it happen at my very first job was certainly not what I expected—it was a huge downfall, from Phi Beta Kappa graduate one year to 'fired failure' the next, in my mind."

When twentysomethings realize that their achievements in college will not necessarily translate to anything in the working world, they can be left wondering why they went to college in the first place. "Phi Beta Kappa" may look impressive on a piece of paper, but it won't automatically bring happiness and success to a graduate. Celia, a 29-year-old in Richmond, Virginia, reached the point where she was so desperate for a job—any job—that she accepted a position for which she hadn't needed a college degree in the first place. While most of her peers were going to graduate school, Celia was determined to find a way to make a living out of her English degree. She applied to radio stations, public relations agencies, advertising firms, and other companies, but they all wanted the types of real-world experience that she didn't have.

"No one wanted me," she says. "I felt trapped, disappointed, scared, and completely misunderstood. Living with my parents made me feel even more despondent. They were pressuring me to get a job, one that had nothing to do with my field. My mother started saying things like, 'Sometimes we have to do things we don't want to do to survive. Work is work—it is not supposed to be fun.' Our relationship began to deteriorate, and I was becoming really confused about what I wanted to do. I had wanted to find steady work as a writer in some sort of corporate-type environment, but with my parents grilling me each day about my search, that goal started to fade."

Eventually, Celia felt pressured to take a job from a family friend who was a corporate manager for a grocery store chain. As an assistant manager assigned to a supermarket bakery/deli, she wore a store uniform, a back brace, and a hat. She cooked chickens, baked doughnuts, fried food, and sliced deli meat. "It was so embarrassing, but I felt obligated to stick it out for my parents and because I needed the money. My boyfriend was still in college, living in the fraternity house. He gave me zero support. I was ashamed of my new job, having graduated with kids working for Intel, IBM, and going on to law school or medical school. I basically lied about my job—not telling him or his friends how my 'management' position forced me to mop floors, pour Cokes, and ring a register. It seemed too depressing to cop to having been the former all-American sorority girl, RA, and admissions counselor at one of the snobbiest Pac Ten schools in the country," Celia says. "I suffered in silence. I began retreating from girlfriends and social situations. I retreated from my parents, too. I'd stay away at work and then head to the fraternity house to hang until my folks were well asleep. My life consisted of frying chicken and counseling frat boys on the ways of women. I didn't know where the old me was, the girl who had control of her life, achieved what she set out to do, and was respected by peers. I lived in the illusion of how the frat boys remembered me in my college prime. I was pathetic—so pathetic that I eventually left the grocery store to take a job with America West Airlines. It was a glamorous little job that promised I'd be flying the friendly skies in a matter of months. Whew—the family would be happy, the friends would be impressed, and I would have made something of myself, despite my English degree and lack of graduate school. 'Whew' turned into 'wow,' which turned into 'what?' and eventually left me wondering what the hell I was doing there. I hit rock bottom."

One day, a former sorority adviser saw Celia behind the airline counter and told her how sad she looked, "all made up in my airline digs." This reflection of her hit home. Within a week, Celia accepted a technical writing job with her former adviser's friends that put her English degree and her love of writing to good use. "Did I expect it would be a more carefree and easy road to where I am now? Yes. I did," she says. "I lived in the illusion of what I was and what I did in college, and it was painful for me to see that these accomplishments were nothing in the real world. I thought I'd be acknowledged and rewarded for my skills long before I was ever even able to put myself somewhere where I'd want a pat on the back."

Phil, a 1997 graduate of Gordon College (Wenham, Massachusetts), had similar expectations; at the very least, he thought he'd receive the acknowledgment he deserved for his work. But instead, he discovered the frustrations of office politics. "I was discouraged a lot. I saw someone who didn't know as much as me and whose quality of work was less than mine, who was advancing more than I was, and that person was my boss," he says. "That made me really upset, because he was also an asshole. I was working really hard and doing stuff and he was getting all the credit and I had been too naive to figure that out, so it was too late. By the time I figured it out, I was unhappy with my job and the person I was working for. As a result, I was very depressed. I lashed out, being sarcastic, bitter, and disgruntled. I was even rude to the people who meant well. It was unhealthy for me and the people I worked with. I was really sour."

Office politics are generally inescapable in any field, but certain lines of work may be more damaging to twentysomethings' self esteem than others. "As an actor, there have been a lot of down moments. I often would question my self-worth and my skills and wonder if I was doing the right thing," says Mark, a 29-year-old in New York City. "Los Angeles is a miserable place to be a struggling actor. Actors get no respect ('Oh, you're an actor—what restaurant do you work in?'), and that wears on your soul. Eventually, I was missing my family, my friends who I grew up with, and my hometown of New York. I think once I hit my mid-twenties and was no longer in that postcollege whirlwind, I had some time to reflect on my years out of college. A few things started happening. I realized I had 'needs'—stability, a home, nice meals, a girlfriend. Also, I realized I could be a struggling actor for twenty years and never catch a break."

Many recent graduates dread the idea that they will never catch a break, while at the same time they wait and wait for something to happen to them that will change their lives. But by waiting and hoping instead of acting, they only set themselves up for a harder fall, says Lynn, a 1995 graduate of Arizona State University (Tempe). "After graduate school, I decided to travel through Europe for what was supposed to be a couple months, but I kept extending my plane ticket and avoiding the real world. I ended up there for six months because I had this attitude like I had nothing to go back to—my stuff was in boxes at my parents' garage and I had no place to live, no boyfriend, and I had said goodbye to all my friends in Boston. It was a little weird and scary because I didn't have anything to go back to, so I avoided the transition by staying in Europe."

When she finally did return, Lynn planned to stay at her parents' house while she commenced her job search. "I had culture shock, and I had to figure out what I wanted to do, and I didn't have any real-world experience. So I was having trouble getting jobs. The jobs that I wanted were above what I was able to be hired to do. My master's is in flute performance, so employers didn't look at it as a real master's," she says. "I was on this extended vacation, so I was refusing to realize that I needed to do something. I was sleeping in and watching TV all day. I kept telling everyone I was working on my résumé and applying for jobs, but it had really slowed down. I think I was in denial that I wasn't really where I was supposed to be. I was giving myself some time as an excuse. I was doing less, getting less motivated. One day I was sitting in my bathrobe at four P.M., Oprah was on, and I was looking at the employment ads thinking, 'God, I'm really pathetic,' in my parents' house in my bathrobe and slippers. I had to wake up and take a look at myself."

Social Adjustments

Another major cause of depression among twentysomethings is the drastic change in social life after graduation. Ed, a 26-year-old living in Santa Barbara, California, says that after college, he felt a large void because he no longer had access to the social outlets he had relied on for four years. "Aside from the people I was working with, I didn't really have anyone, so it was really isolated. If you let it get to you, you can get really depressed because you're used to this level of interaction and all of a sudden it goes away," he says. "I have gone through a couple of long phases of doubts. The times where you feel like you don't have a large degree of control over your schedule are the toughest. You feel like giving up on the whole thing, because that seems to be the solution. All of this has been compounded by my lack of ability to meet women. In my experience the best way to do that is through friends of friends, but in Santa Barbara I don't have so many connections through which I could accomplish this. Not that there's a lack of attractive women here, but the means I might have to meet them are quite limited. So if anything has gotten me the most depressed, it's been my inability to meet interesting, intelligent, and not just attractive women."

Samantha, a 25-year-old from Minneapolis, also had trouble adjusting to the change in her social life after graduation. Throughout college, she focused most of her attention on the groups and activities with which she was involved. She valued her college friends, but they all had other interests that kept them from becoming too socially and emotionally dependent on each other. "My early to mid-twenties have been a difficult time for me. My ideas about relationships, especially friendship, have drastically changed as I've learned more about myself and what I want and need from people," she says. "After graduation, there was no focus in my life. I didn't know what kind of career I wanted and there were no organized activities that I was interested in joining. I felt like I should still be in college, that I was younger than the people at work, and was midway between being a young adult and an adult. I found solace in my roommates, creating a surrogate family that I could focus on so that I could avoid dealing with my insecurity and fear. They seemed to have the same need, and we spent more and more time with each other. Going out every night and planning elaborate activities and trips with my roommates became the constant in my life. We all had a need to know everything about each others' lives and form a family unit with each other."

But gradually, instead of helping her to escape her problems, Samantha's roommates became her problem. "We started to resent each other for the closeness we tried so hard to achieve. I never saw myself as needing very much personal space, but I think it was something I always took for granted. Although I never saw myself as someone who would ever need therapy, I started seeing it as an attractive option," she says. "It was hard to discuss problems with my 'family' of roommates, as my problems mostly focused on my relationships with them. Therapy became *my* time to talk about *my* feelings and not have to qualify anything. I think as I grew older, I realized that I don't have to deal with everything perfectly, and sometimes I might need help figuring out feelings and reactions I have. Although I don't know how long I will continue therapy, it has been invaluable in helping me deal with my changing needs and issues."

Overwhelming Factors

Sometimes twentysomethings can feel as if their world is caving in on them, not just because they doubt everything at once, but because things actually happen to them all at once and they don't have the experience or capacity to deal with them. Colin, a 23-year-old living in Manchester, New Hampshire, says he fell into a depression both because he couldn't handle all of the things that were going on in his life and because somehow he was expected to be able to. As a musician and a writer trying to find his place in a society that is predominantly nine to five, Colin says he had a hard time with the transition pretty much as soon as he graduated. "There's this whole thing of being in a bubble for twenty-one years where you don't really have this real life.

It's very easy to be an artist when you're in college. Then you get out and you have to figure out a way to substantiate your life as an artist, which is very difficult. I lived with my aunt in Boston right after graduation, so I was trying to make a progression and not just a drastic change. But then I had this relationship with a girl in New York, so I moved to New York and did music, but too many things bombarded me at once and I couldn't quite keep it together," Colin says. "Our relationship ended not because she was 26 and I was 23, but because she was having the same problems trying to focus, so there was that, plus finding a place and a job in New York City, and then the monetary problems, and it was just absolutely overbearing. I took it all out on myself. My parents were a humongous support system, but I talked to them all the time, and they'd tell me, 'Oh, I was there; everyone goes through it; it's part of life; it's growing; you'll see in hindsight one day; you'll look back and this period will be not a negative but a positive thing; it taught you a valuable lesson.' I would call up and be crying and miserable, because my life for two years was with this girl, I moved to New York for her, and all of a sudden it was over. She was my life for two years, and then I was in this big city where I knew no one. I'd sit on the kitchen floor—with no furniture just a phone—in Brooklyn. I was going through this part alone, which was not good because I thought that I wasn't adequate, that I couldn't perform, and that something was wrong with me when it wasn't true."

Two months after his breakup, Colin, who was trying to be a singer-songwriter, decided he couldn't deal with his depression alone anymore. "I called up my dad and completely broke down. I had been miserable trying to deal with this, having a broken heart in New York City, trying to get situated. So I called him and he said, 'You know what, you need to come home, remember who you are, and get strong.' So he picked me up and brought me back home yesterday. I'm not manic-depressive, but I'm more along those lines than I am stream-lined. I have ups and downs," he says. "The instability is kind of tough if you're not ready. It's so much easier to dream when you're in college. When you get out, a lot of things get put out in front of your dreams and you can't see that anymore, and when that happens you lose that light and energy that you need to achieve your dreams. And you can't see them because of 'do this, do that, pay the bills, find a place, find a job, your girlfriend left you, you're in a new place, you don't have a support system here.' And I was definitely having a hard time remembering what I wanted to do. Within those parameters, you can fall very, very low and it's all about the moment, and you have to remember it's just the moment and not forever. And happiness is what I want to find in life—that's all I'm looking for, because if you can find that, what else really matters? But I've always had to struggle with that."

The feeling that peers are moving more quickly toward a stable adulthood while a twentysomething wallows, alone and stagnant, is a common complaint. Maura, a 1995 graduate of Johns Hopkins University (Baltimore), says that she tries to ease her doubts by comparing herself to other people, but that sort of analysis only makes her feel worse. "I get these moments when I feel like I'm completely far behind, like everyone else is ahead of me, like I'm not where I should be in terms of relationships, friends, jobs. It's like a continuing cycle of doubts. I'll go to a couple's place and see their beautiful sofa and a living room that looks like a Pottery Barn catalogue and feel like I'm going to be living alone in my apartment for the rest of my life," she says. "I don't know when it will end. Sometimes I wonder how long it is going to take before I don't burst into tears every time I get my student loan bill. There are certainly moments when I lose it. It's a long and painful road. When it's especially rough on me, I have those doubts."

Maura says she thinks the twenties can trigger such stinging self-criticism because recent graduates have nothing to hold onto as some unwavering measure of their self-worth. "It has a lot to do with trying to accomplish different sections of your life at once. College is like an anchor and when you graduate, that's taken away. It's scary not to know how permanent things are anymore," she says. "In high school, you have all of these dreams, and you just figure you'll be married with kids. But after graduation, you get a more realistic idea of what your life will be like. You learn how hard it is to get there and how depressing it can be. Being able to get married and have kids is not the easiest thing in the world." The most difficult period for Maura was when she moved alone to New York City in an effort to jumpstart her career, because she also had to worry about setting up a new social structure. "It was so hard, so hard to move. It took one and a half years before I had any friends—and I was lucky because I had my best friend living next door. But he already had his life set up. It's hard in New York because once they are established here, people are so social and busy, and when you're home renting movies every night it's so depressing. It was the fear of the unknown, the 'Oh my God, it's not all going to work out' feeling. I figured of course I'd make friends—it would be ridiculous to think I wouldn't—but then a year went by and I was left thinking, 'Where are they?' It starts to get scary."

As the years add up after graduation, twentysomethings can feel increasing amounts of pressure if the life they had hoped for doesn't seem to be panning out. Ashley, a 1997 graduate of Brown University (Providence, Rhode Island), says that, even though she is only 25, she feels like the time she has to set up her life is beginning to run out. "I feel more lost now than when I first graduated. Now I feel pressured to make decisions for the rest of my life. Now I'm thinking if I go to business school I can't wait much longer, and will I get married, and all those questions. So much of it is out of my control—and it's harder to figure out what's under control. I'm scared I'll go down one path too far and won't be able to switch. In the commercial for the Bruce Willis movie *The Kid*, they ask you, 'When you were eight years old, could you imagine yourself doing what you do today?' I couldn't, and hope this isn't what I'm going to be doing for the rest of my life. Lately I've definitely been feeling more lost. Everything is unsettled. If you think about it, our parents were married by the time they were our age. They were on track. And I'm not happy with where I live because lately I have been feeling like I'm older than everyone I know. I'm living with a bunch of guys who still think they're in college. It's suddenly hitting me now that I'm older than them. I'm also not happy with my job. I went to this new job which I thought would be exciting and it's ended up being a real disappointment. I like being at a company around a lot of young people, but I feel like I have to ask permission to go to the bathroom. Do I want to stay in this area? I have no idea about anything. I don't think anyone has anything figured out. I look at my superiors at work, and they're just stumbling along too. I feel like everyone's stumbling around."

Anchors Aweigh

Maura's description of college as an anchor—and graduation as having that anchor abruptly snatched away—is echoed by many twentysomethings. Leaving college is a little bit like riding a bicycle for the first time—except it's not just that a trusted adult lets go of the bike at a certain time once the twentysomething has learned how to steady himself while moving forward. It's more like the bicycle suddenly disappears. Justin, a 24-year-old living in Boston, says that for him, college meant comfort—and when he graduated, the stability and security he had developed in school seemed to drop out from under him. "I was having this postpartum-like depression because my college was my life— all of my friends were from there. I only had a couple of friends from high school and my close friends all moved away, but a lot were in the same position as me. They didn't know what they were going to do, didn't want to go to graduate school right away, but were just taking whatever job they could take," he says. "I always felt like a loser, because I went to a pretty good school and I wasn't being paid very well at my job, which I took because it was the first one that came along. So I felt really guilty that I wasted my parents' money on that. I felt out of control, like my life was completely out of my hands and I didn't know what to do with myself. And even now I still kind of feel that way. I'm trying to get a handle on it, but it's really hard to separate myself from my college. When I drive by, I think, 'What I would give for just one more year there.' I think it would be easier in another city because when I see my school, I want to go back, where it was safe. I felt safe there because I didn't have to make any life decisions that were going to turn out disastrously."

To make matters even more complex, on top of all of the other twentysomething anxieties, Justin says he also has to learn how to become comfortable with his sexuality in a world that is much bigger than his school. "I didn't come out until my senior year of college. I wasn't into any of the gay associations at school, and it took me a while to be ready to acknowledge it. But in college when people found out, as I got more comfortable and told everyone, I felt very safe. I felt like the campus was open and liberal enough that I wouldn't get gay-bashed or anything. Granted, not everyone's open about it, but in general I felt okay," he says. "It's harder to deal with in the real world—growing up I didn't know anyone gay. Going into the new job and not being in that safe environment was a little sketchy. I didn't know how the real world would react to it, because the microcosm of college is a lot different from the real world. It's still hard. I'm not a hundred percent completely comfortable with it. I don't have that many gay friends, and I'm still really skittish around gay people, which is so odd. Especially around gay men, I'm uncomfortable. I lose my confidence with them. The gay world is all about being glammed up and wearing expensive clothes. I don't really care about that. I went to a couple of clubs, which was a bad scene because it's like fresh meat—people are out to use you and that's not a good thing. People I've met recently are all about appearances, but there are a lot more important things than that. I'm a lot more comfortable with it now, but the town I come from is very rural, redneck, and homophobic. Also my best friend from home is gay, and I can't deal with the rumors."

Like Justin, Courtney, a 25-year-old in Des Moines, remained in her college town for a while after graduation. She had expected that living near her school would ease her transition, but she soon found out—also like Justin—that she had only made it more difficult for herself to let go. "I had this incredible college experience for four years, and then the city and environment didn't change, but my entire life changed. It was harder for me to adjust from going from college to the real world, because my physical surroundings were constant. It felt like a different place, and it was frustrating because we had lived in such a self-contained campus and I didn't know the city that well. All of a sudden, when I said I lived in that city, I actually lived there," she says. "It was very disheartening to hear about all of my friends who had moved. We were all going through new experiences, but it was the hardest for me because I kept driving by the places that we used to hang out. I was left behind in this know-nothing city. I had my whole new life ahead of me that I was there to enjoy and pursue, but it was that much harder because I didn't have a clean break from my college life."

For Courtney, the hardest part of her transition was the realization that all of the guidelines that led her up to and then through college simply didn't have any counterparts in the real world. The routines and goals of academic life didn't translate into anything after graduation. "I was scared a lot because school was very easy—not always academically, but you knew the rules and knew how to get by and not flounder. It was a game and if you knew how to play the game, you knew you were going to be okay. But this whole career and serious working thing was so remote to me. I didn't understand it and I didn't know what to do or how I was supposed to act. I tried to give up drinking Coke because I didn't think it was professional—I actually had a conversation with my mom about what I was going to drink at business lunches because I thought I would have to start drinking water and coffee and adult things. I really didn't know anything about it, and it was so scary because I didn't have any kind of a friend base when I started working. It felt like I was going through it all alone. I think one of the things that I found over the last few years that's been interesting to me is that when I first graduated and first started out, I was thinking about 'Is this what I want to do for the rest of my life?' and the answer was always no. So that compounded the feelings of confusion. It's too overwhelming—when people graduate they think about the rest of their lives. And there's no way that you can know what to do for the rest of your life. You can't know. And you'll be a year out of school, a little older, and depressed because you couldn't reach any of the goals you set for yourself. Reality knocks you down to your knees."

Life after graduation walloped Carly, a 28-year-old from Atlanta, because she had been so successful in school. She had an athletic scholarship and worked as a waitress during college, but she didn't really keep track of where her money went, and she tried not to think about how she would support herself after graduation. "I thought I was very important in college and that I would go on to do great things, like write the great American novel. And then I really became very depressed in knowing that I don't think I had the maturity for it. I don't think I knew what that all meant. I was totally unprepared for life after college."

After graduation, Carly got some money from her father, which she quickly spent on groceries. She started to charge everything on her credit card, but that only made things worse. Because she couldn't afford to go to Europe as she had hoped, she came up with the alternate adventure of working on an Indian reservation in Oregon. But living in a shack in the middle of the desert with no car and no phone didn't quite lessen her stress, so she moved to Los Angeles. "That time in L.A., especially at the start, was really hard because in college I was successful with my studies and my athletics. I really had very little concept of the fact that I wasn't going to become successful so easily after college, where I had that structure set up for me with which to plug in whatever skills I had. Then, after college, that structure wasn't set up for me anymore and I was at a complete loss. I had to pay car insurance, and health insurance, and rent, and computer payments. I had zero direction, and I still think I don't have direction," she says. "I started drinking a lot. I really hit a low emotionally and it all spiraled down from there because it was so emotionally stressful. I started reaching out for things in the past, like ex-boyfriends, and I really became very, very depressed. It was a very difficult time for me. I gained weight. I knew that it was because I wasn't exercising, I was drinking too much, and smoking too much."

Even though she had a relatively fun job in development and television as an assistant at a large corporation, it wasn't enough of an anchor. Carly tried to cling to her past as a way of grounding her identity, which she felt was whirling out of her control. "I absolutely doubted myself because all of a sudden I was answering telephones and scheduling massages and schmoozing in L.A., this world where you had to become friends with the right people and look a certain way even to go to the laundromat. And I made a conscious effort not to buy into all of that, but I think it was unavoidable to some degree. I felt like who I was before I moved to L.A. and graduated from college was sort of lost. I was an English department geek and loved going to teas and readings, and then all of a sudden I had no way of knowing how to apply that to my real life," she says. "I think it's important for people to know that everyone is going through this. Because I felt like a freak. I was surrounded by people who were really ambitious, who had gone to film school. I had no idea what I wanted. I'd find myself getting in my car after work, buying a six-pack of beer, and going home and watching the Thursday night lineup. Before the night was over, three or four of the beers would be finished, and I'd end up writing some pathetic letter to some ex-boyfriend and then falling asleep. And then getting up the next day and doing the same thing. And really feeling like there was no end in sight to that, like there was no end. That's what it was. That's just what the 'real world' was."

Dashed Expectations

A major factor of the quarterlife crisis is that real life does not turn out to be what many twentysomethings expect. It isn't just that college does not actually prepare students for the years beyond graduation. For all of their lives, twentysomethings have been told that they can be whatever they want to be, do whatever they want to do—which was great to hear when they were formulating childhood dreams and aspirations. But once they get to the point where it is time to make those goals happen, twentysomethings often realize that not everything is attainable. The resulting feeling is something like what happens to Charlie Brown in the *Peanuts* comic strip, when he takes a running start to kick the football, and at the last minute Lucy pulls the ball away so that Charlie Brown falls flat on his back.

For all of her life, Julie, a 1995 graduate of the University of Maryland (College Park), had banked on becoming a judge, but when she took a paralegal job, she says it slowly washed over her that she didn't want to pursue law anymore. "I was an extremely confident and ambitious teen. I always knew what I wanted and I got everything I wanted. Then I left college and nothing was for sure anymore. Almost immediately I found out that everything I thought I was going to do was wrong, like it had all been a joke and people were just putting up with me," she says. "I tried to compensate for being unhappy by buying stuff, spending money I didn't have. I was miserable. I would go out at night, buy clothes. It was just awful and I felt terrible. I was like, 'Who am I fooling?' I needed to figure out something else but I didn't know what it was. I was starting over at 24."

George, a 1999 graduate of St. Norbert College (DePere, Wisconsin), says that his troubles began when he just assumed that things would naturally fall into place after college. "Things only got worse after graduation. I had resolutely refused to make plans for graduate school, believing that I could quickly get a job, settle down, work at getting published, knit back together the rapidly unraveling strands of my life. It didn't happen," he says. "I moved back home. I was lonely and sad. My friends from high school were gone. My college friends had dispersed, pursuing their own lives, leaving me in limbo. I was too old to be living on a par with my younger sibs, too old to be under my parents' authority, but too immature, evidently, to get a job, my own place, my own life. How the battlements of my poor self-esteem crumbled. After a year, I cracked under the pressure."

It's not unusual for a twentysomething's self-esteem to falter because of these dashed expectations. Ken, a 29-year old living in San Diego, expected to get his master's degree and then move back home, where he could live close to his friends and family. "But that hasn't happened because my job is in technology and they don't have technology at home, so it has been quite emotional. As soon as graduate school ended it slapped me in the face, the reality of being there with virtually no friends. I'm still dealing with that. It's something I have to come to peace with: that you're in an area that's best for your profession, not best for your personal life, which you have to break away from—from the family life and what you know, and just go with the things that are not certain," he says. "It was overwhelming, because I was working, looking for other work, and trying to learn to deal with the emotional stress of not really being in a job I liked at the time, not really knowing where I fit into the corporate world. I think the stress was the biggest thing for me: learning to look for jobs while you're at a job without burning bridges. That affected me physically, too—I gained weight."

For Greg, a 1993 graduate of Georgetown University (Washington, D.C.), dashed expectations led to settling for an uninspiring job because he was faced with financial realities he had not anticipated. Greg expected that he would go straight from college to graduate school, thereby postponing his entrance into the real world for at least a few years. But when he didn't get into any schools, he didn't know what else to do besides parlay his summer job into a full-time position. "It was a rushed deal for me because I had not gotten my résumé together, so the summer job turned into a career. I went through some hard times because I wasn't ready for it. I got myself into some budgeting troubles the first couple of years. Things got kind of out of control. I went back to some of my high school friends and discovered I really didn't have much in common with them, so I ended up hanging out with my two brothers. I tried to maintain a long-distance relationship, which had its rocky moments and was not so successful. There were times where I would drive back to school in the fall, because I missed going back. It was such a habit going back every fall. I found after a couple years I didn't really fit in there any more," he says. "I was disappointed with the real world. There were so many things when I got out of college that I wanted to do. And they were all superceded by financial things that needed to be taken care of first, such as school loans, rent, getting a car, and things I wanted to do, like go to Europe for a month. I never did that. I had some basic regrets that I didn't do more traveling before I got married."

Financial concerns are often a driving force behind dashed expectations because many college students don't realize the impact that money (or lack of it) will have on their after-college lives. Olivia, a 2000 graduate of Dalhousie University (Halifax, Nova Scotia), says she expected the months after graduation to be exciting and adventurous—exactly the opposite of what she is currently experiencing. "I always envisioned postcollege life as a time of uninhibited freedom. I would travel the country and the world; I would hold a variety of interesting and challenging jobs; I would meet new people and make new friends," she says. "But travel requires money, and I won't have any money until I secure a job. So here I am at home, living with my parents, working at my old summer job where I do nothing more interesting than stacking CDs on shelves. I feel like instead of progressing forward into more freedom, more opportunity, and a more interesting life, I slid backward. It's like I'm still in college, except without the college part to look forward to. It's almost like being in high school again. I know I can move out as soon as I am offered and accept a job, but despite the assurances of well-meaning adults that 'this is the best job market in years,' no job seems forthcoming. I grow increasingly despairing and hopeless as I languish in a sea of boredom. Who wouldn't be easily frustrated in this position?"

As a result of the postgraduation letdown—the realization that life is not going to be what she had envisioned—Olivia says she is going through a tough emotional period. "Now that I have graduated from college, I have noticed some changes in my emotions. My temper seems shorter and I am more easily frustrated. My ambivalent station in life puts me in a precarious position, where even little occurrences can tip my emotional scales. Lately I snap and get frustrated easily," she says. "This transition puts me on edge. I just feel so anxious all the time, so eager to begin the next phase of my life, and I feel like I'm taking a step backwards when I should be taking a step forward, and I don't know if I'm going to break out of that feeling until I move out of the house, have a job, and live somewhere new. My job doesn't help, because it's pretty boring. You feel like you have this B.A., you know so much now, you've developed your brain cells, and here you are putting CDs on the shelf."

Paradise Lost

All of these factors—intense self-doubt, problems with learning a new work or social protocol, being overwhelmed by everything happening at once, losing the college anchor, dashed expectations—can contribute to the sense of helplessness that many twentysomethings feel in the years after graduation. Several twentysomethings told us the best way to describe this feeling is to say they feel lost, hopeless, and clueless, which can trigger or prolong a precarious emotional period. "After graduation, I didn't have any real plans," says Sandra, a 25-year-old in Birmingham, Alabama. "I figured I would just go home and live in the town I grew up in, and the thought depressed me. In fact, I got so upset that I started crying nonstop—I mean, literally, I couldn't stop crying."

Jon, a 1992 graduate of Rutgers University (New Brunswick, New Jersey), had a similar feeling of cluelessness after school ended. "I had absolutely no idea what I wanted to do right out of college. I was clueless and fell blindly into a couple dead end jobs, which were just there for me to make money and figure out what I wanted to do. When I had no idea what I wanted to do, I couldn't even picture myself doing anything because I was so clueless about what was out there. I had so little direction. I was hanging onto these completely dead-end jobs thinking that maybe something would turn up. I was unhappy about the situation, and the only thing that made it better was that all of my friends out of college were in the same boat. We would all come home and complain about our jobs together. We were all still drunks back then."

Because Rich, a 25-year-old from San Francisco, didn't know what he wanted to do with his life after college, he followed his friends to graduate school to study physical therapy. After two and a half years, he realized that he didn't want to become a physical therapist, so he had to start again from scratch. He moved back home to do some temp work while he tried to figure out what to do next. "Living at home was not going to work for me. My friends were all working, and I was still there, and I'm pretty independent myself, but being independent by nature and living under the same roof as your mom doesn't work too well. It's one of the most frustrating things. You're in a job and it's your job, but it's not what you're going to end up doing, but you're still stuck there thinking. You're already comfortable getting your paycheck, and you know it's not what you want to do, but it's hard to make yourself actually do it," he says. "I thought all of a sudden I was put into such a strange environment where I had all these responsibilities: my student loans were kicking in, I had to make rent, I had to prove to myself that I could be truly independent, and that was something that I wasn't sure if I could do or handle by myself. At the same time, all my friends from PT school were finding jobs doing what I had been trained to do but had chosen not to. I felt that at that moment my life was useless. I felt that for all intents and purposes, I had no skills worth marketing for a new job, since the one skill that I had I would not use. At the same time, I had absolutely no idea what I wanted to do. During the time I was living with my mom, I remember that everything just hit me then: here I was with six years of college and postcollege education and I was doing data entry."

As Amy explained when she paraphrased Socrates earlier in this chapter, twentysomethings often look for change as a way to run away from the problems they are facing (which, to make things more complicated, are many times sparked by change in the first place). Rich tried to address his feeling of hopelessness by moving out of his mother's house, but found that his hopelessness moved with him. "I really got a little depressed then and felt very useless. I felt myself getting stupider with every stupid address that I entered into those computers," he says. "I was depressed when I was living with my mom, because I felt that I was not doing anything with my life and I wanted to be so independent but I couldn't yet. That was the most frustrating thing. You have the luxury of feeling totally independent in college, yet in reality it is only because of all the loans and parental support. Once all that is gone, you really think twice. It really was a shock for me to have to go back home. Now, living by myself, I still get very anxious. I want to find the job I am 'meant to be in.' I get lonely when I come back from work, since this is the first time I am living alone."

Rachel, a 1994 graduate of Mary Washington College (Fredericksburg, Virginia), also went to graduate school because she didn't know what else to do. She directly attributes her ensuing depression to this strange lost feeling, which graduate school didn't alleviate. "The transition was really difficult—I didn't know what to do with myself at all, and coming out with a bachelor's degree I felt like I couldn't get a high-enough paying job," she says. "It was really hard after college ended. I didn't want to stay home with my family in New Jersey, and with the social changes, it was just the feeling of being completely lost and not knowing where to go or who to live with. I felt like graduate school was one of my only options, because at least it put me somewhere different, and I would make social contacts through that, and then hopefully it would help me to find a better job that I couldn't find with my bachelor's degree. So I went to graduate school without really thinking it through. I just made the decision to move because I really wanted to move somewhere. Moving to a new city was also really huge and difficult. Meeting people, finding friends and where to live and who to live with, were huge problems. Often I was hit with these feelings that I was just not happy."

Now, two years out of graduate school, Rachel still doesn't know what she should be doing with her life. As she gets older, she worries increasingly about how she will handle all of the various aspects of being an adult when her first instinct was to put off adulthood for as long as possible. "I've had feelings of hopelessness, loneliness, and isolation throughout my twenties, on and off," she says. "Sometimes a job will temporarily relieve that, but not really. I'm unhappier now more than ever. There's no support group or anything for groups of people in their twenties to get together and discuss this stuff. I've been through a lot, going from a group house, which is an interesting experience, then going into an apartment and having to find a roommate, and now living by myself. And I've had a lot of friends who have come and gone because this city is so transient. On top of all of that, there's the pressure to find someone and have a romantic relationship work out."

Trying Out Therapy

The notion of seeking professional help for their distressing feelings does not always occur to twentysomethings, for at least a couple of reasons. First, many recent graduates associate therapy with a certain stigma. Because therapy is not something that their peers generally discuss, twentysomethings think it is unusual for people their age to seek that kind of guidance. Furthermore, therapy isn't cheap. By the time they graduate from college, most twentysomethings can no longer be covered by their parents' health insurance; indeed, many twentysomethings forgo health insurance entirely. Without that kind of coverage, the cost of seeing a psychologist is, not surprisingly, prohibitive, particularly when a person's main concern is how to scrounge up enough money to pay the rent.

But some twentysomethings do turn to mental health professionals during this strange limbo period, and some say that the therapy helped. "I saw a therapist for the first year I was out of college, which was essential to overcoming my self-doubts and depression," says Denise, a 1996 graduate of Yale University (New Haven, Connecticut). "She showed me that the doubts I feel are related to what I am, in any given moment, trying to let go of. Old dreams that I realize were not my own. Goals that I have replaced with new ones. When I feel self-doubt I have tools to remind me that the doubts come from inside of me rather than from the real world outside of me."

Todd, a 1997 graduate of Georgia Tech University (Atlanta), says that he sought therapy precisely because he had problems transitioning from college to the real world. "There was a point in my life when I was so stressed out about what was not happening in my life that I knew I needed help. I spent a great deal of my first few years out of school realizing that I did not have the kind of young-adult support group that any person needs when they leave college. (By young-adult support group, I mean a set of similarly aged friends who are experiencing the same kinds of 'college-detachment' issues.) I found myself stressing out about where I could find friends, not to mention where I could have dates. Part of the problem was that I felt very needy, and I knew it was because I was afraid to be by myself. I didn't really enjoy my own company, which made me ask how other people could enjoy my company if I didn't even like who I was. A large number of sleepless nights and a lack of appetite convinced me that something needed to happen," he says. "One day, I finally got the guts to call my employer's emotional assistance line. I was surprised to find that there was a compassionate person on the other end of the line who guided me to a counselor. I was worried that the counselor would diagnose me with depression and put me on medication, but I was surprised that, instead, we talked about ways that I needed to relax to control my anxiety. We talked about relaxation techniques and we talked about self-worth. It took time, but I eventually found out that I really enjoy my own company and who I am. When I reached that point, the friends came naturally, since people finally wanted to be around me, instead of me needing to be around them."

Therapy can work for people in different ways. Carly was able to break through her depression because her therapist helped her to look at her life from a different perspective. She only regrets that she waited three years before she sought assistance. "I think seeing the therapist and having a really strong support system was really important to me at the time. In therapy, I learned a lot about the difference between doing and being," she says. "You can imagine how much traffic there is in L.A. I would sit in my car and space out and fantasize about all these great things I was going to do and how I was going to look, and none of it was real. And then I'd go back to my small life and feel even more depressed. I got to the point where I didn't leave the house a whole lot. So my therapist helped me by talking about my fantasies. And finally it was about doing things instead of fantasizing about them: if you want to be in shape, then wake up in the morning and go for a walk. (That's oversimplifying it; it took a long time to make this work for me.) Or instead of being in the car and fantasizing about what I wanted to do in ten years, she taught me to say, 'What am I doing now? I'm in this car, behind another car on the 405, driving into the Valley'—to really stay in the present, because otherwise I felt very far away."

Emily, a 22-year-old in Los Angeles, was skeptical about how a therapist could help her get through rough periods in her life. "I felt it was a rite of passage. I did not see what a therapist could do for me, since I already spent most of my time obsessing and thinking about myself in one way or another. What could he or she say that I haven't said? What could they figure out that I couldn't? And besides, I'm so smart and intuitive myself, I'll probably end up dissecting and analyzing *them*. I'll show them that they can't analyze me! They can't solve this! I'm sure of it," she says. "So I marched into the office with raised eyebrows and a very sure sense of what was wrong (particularly middle-school instances and the loss of my virginity, which I was positive were to blame). I rattled off my theories as to why I am this way and then instructed my therapist that I would like it to stop *immediately*. I waited, assuming he would tell me something that was worth an hourly rate and would clear up the issues in my head. I mean, I was paying him to help, was I not? He didn't tell me anything or say anything; he merely asked me questions. I thought I knew where he was headed, and perhaps I actually did. But as I talked, I also listened. When I was ready, a few sessions later, I was willing to admit things I didn't want to admit and discuss what I didn't want to discuss. Therapy is hard. It's terribly, frustratingly, furiously hard. Although since it isn't a college exam or moving a refrigerator, this kind of challenge is not easy to pinpoint. I went for twelve sessions and never solved anything; however, I progressed greatly. When I can afford it, I'm going back ASAP."

Emily explains that having this detached third party take an objective look at her life made it somewhat easier for her to do the same. As a result, her doubts about herself eased a little bit, in part because she was starting to understand why she was having them in the first place. "Contrary to popular belief, a therapist isn't someone we pay to be a friend because we are too much of a loser to have any friends. A therapist—a good therapist (you must shop and compare like a consumer, mind you)—is someone we pay to make sense of our thoughts," she says. "No one thinks anything of paying a personal trainer, or a gym, or a dentist, or a foot doctor, or a nutritionist. For me, my doubts about myself clouded me, brought me down, and came on unexpectedly. A therapist helped me find the source and start whacking at it. Everyone is different; everyone has different sources of mental and emotional pains or imbalances; but unhappiness is unacceptable—especially when it is unhappiness with one's self."

Victoria, a 25-year-old New Yorker, says that she valued this outside perspective, despite the negative way her peers reacted when she confided to them that she had seen a therapist. "I chose to see a psychologist because I was breaking down mentally. I couldn't figure out what everything meant on my own. It becomes difficult to make logical decisions when you are emotionally distraught. Therapy really helped me to focus my thoughts so I could then make the decisions that I felt were best for me. It takes work, and if you're willing to tackle your weaknesses it can be very beneficial. Yes, you could talk to a family member or friend about what's going on, but getting an objective viewpoint that challenges your intellect and emotion can be more helpful," she says. "But there's a stigma attached to psychotherapy. People who have never tried it tend to see it as a weakness or something that's trendy. I didn't always receive a positive response when I confided to certain friends that I've been in therapy. As someone who turned to therapy when she most desperately needed it, I can honestly say it works. I don't see a therapist presently, but if I ever needed it again, I would definitely take advantage of it. I have since presented peers with the option of psychotherapy and have advised them to take the plunge."

The stigma attached to therapy and antidepressants leads many twentysomethings to consider the subjects taboo, even with friends. As a result, because twentysomethings don't discuss them, they naturally assume that it is uncommon for people their age to need them. This assumption can make the quarterlife crisis worse when twentysomethings don't do anything to help themselves simply because they don't know or cannot accept their options. Ryan, a 28-year-old in Crystal Lake, Illinois, says his sense of emotional well-being deteriorated because of a disappointing job and a frustrating living arrangement at home with his parents. "I found myself less and less willing to go out, not wanting to get out of bed to go to a job that I didn't like anymore, and more and more likely to be upset about useless, trivial things. This was not my normal, outgoing self," he says. "I came close to being fired from work for just not putting in the kind of effort I should have at a consulting firm, and took a ton of sick and personal days when they weren't needed. It was not a good situation. It made matters worse that no one I knew had been on antidepressants, except for those anorexic girls and suicidal nutcases in high school. I thought there was some sort of stigma attached to it, and I sure didn't need any pill to make me happier. My dad worked every day and seemed to like it—he's my idol of sorts—so I thought I should slog through it, too. That didn't work. Life was miserable and it was ruining my friendships. Finally, long after I should have, I saw a shrink, a nice guy who never once said, 'Tell me about your mother.' Thank God, because that's a whole other book in itself. But the drugs worked. Slowly, amazingly, I 'woke up' and came back to an even keel. I was open with my close friends about what was up, but they didn't quite accept it until each one of them went through the same thing. All six of my closest friends came to me, one after another, asking for total confidentiality and wondering about the drugs. We're now a Prozac group. Each has been on for the minimum three-month dosage to get us back to normal. Each of us coupled it with major changes in our lifestyles. I left my job, started working for myself, and got on a career track that has been amazing, and I haven't fallen into that depression crap again."

Brushing It Off

There are ways that twentysomethings can get through this incredibly difficult part of the quarterlife crisis without resorting to therapy. But twentysomethings told us that their success pretty much depended on one of two things: what kind of luck they had in the various areas of their lives; or how well they could hold themselves together to keep up the right kind of attitude. The twentysomethings with the most positive outlooks were inevitably the ones who believed their doubts were normal.

Brandon, a 24-year-old in Los Angeles, explained to us how this kind of attitude has helped him cope with his post-graduation fears and uncertainties: accepting his self-doubts allows him to brush them off and concentrate on living his life instead. "Doubts mean we're human," he says. "We're supposed to have a bit of doubt. I don't necessarily think that therapy is the correct answer. Some things will go right; some things will go wrong. That's what life is all about. I don't know if the doubt is the part that is the most worrisome. I think it's probably the idea that no one else really feels all that sorry for you. And why should they? It seems fairly rare that someone goes through life without ever knowing what it's like to find a poop stain in their underwear, and if you happen to be one of those people, then I feel sorry for you. You should really go see a therapist or something.

"You don't get lectures about what life is like after college. You don't have a textbook that tells you what you need to do to find success. There's no more four-year timetable to decide your friends, your major, your career path. Did my parents spend almost six figures so that I could answer phones all day and fix paper jams? No. I didn't go to college to become a receptionist. But then again, I didn't take a cross-country road trip to become a country music fan, and guess what happened? I saw Garth Brooks in concert in Fargo, North Dakota, and the rest is history.

"You've got to suffer in order to truly appreciate. Be scared. Jump in the water anyway. If it's cold and you get a little shrinkage, so what? If you went with your gut, then you made the right decision. Second-guessing is the worst. *The worst.* I hate it and I hate living my life that way. Maybe we're doubting because we've got less 'control' over our position than we ever have had in the past. So when we get a chance to act, it drives us to the brink of insanity: 'This one decision I make could affect my life for the next dozen years.' That's enough to drive anyone mad. But it's not a healthy way to think. I believe in giving people the benefit of the doubt and giving a new situation every possible chance to be a positive one. But if you make a choice and some time down the road it turns out to be a bad one, you also can't be afraid to move on.

"I think doubting is natural," Brandon says. "The older we get, the more tough choices we have to face. They probably don't get any easier to make, but we can't be afraid to make them, either. Hmm. Maybe I do need a therapist."

five
How Do I Know If the Decisions I'm Making Are the Right Ones?

The doubts and depression that twentysomethings discussed in Chapter 4 often encompass relatively long periods of time, but they don't, in most cases, last forever. The smaller-scale doubts regarding specific decisions twentysomethings have to make, however, can occur on an ongoing, month-to-month or even day-to-day basis. Recent graduates often agonize over their decisions; they can spend months trying to figure out the proper choice—or procrastinating so they don't have to make one in the first place. The problem is twofold. First, young adults often believe that the decisions they make now could possibly alter the course of their lives. So they feel that there is a lot riding on the choices they make. This pressure to make the right decisions can make twentysomethings feel that they need to weigh every side of an option before choosing one. The other reason for these smaller-scale doubts is that recent graduates are supposed to make important decisions when they hardly have any prior experience on which to base their reasoning. If I haven't done this before, a twentysomething reasons, then how do I know I am doing it right?

The pressure on people at this time of life can get intense, but the stress is often something that twentysomethings put on themselves, says Steve, a 22-year-old from Omaha. One of the questions that resonates through the minds of young graduates is whether they should make a decision that will benefit them immediately or set them up for the long term. These long-term versus short-term alternatives do not just revolve around financial investments, although many twentysomethings feel that, because they will be much better off thirty years from now, they will need their money more desperately at this time—to pay back loans, to scrounge for grocery money, to travel—than when they retire. It has been drilled into recent graduates that they need to set themselves up for the future. But that universal warning is just another stressful addition to the swarm of admonishments swirling around in recent graduates' heads.

"It's tricky. I think more than ever that we as a generation know what happens when we make decisions that affect the long term," Steve says. "But there is no 'Live for today because you might not live to see tomorrow.' No 'Do this job because it treats us well.' It's all about where is this going, and am I maximizing my education, skills, and desires? Another tricky thing is 'Am I even qualified to make these decisions?' Give up an opportunity at a great job because I want to have a family life—who am I kidding? I don't even have a wife yet. Invest now for the future—will I even live till tomorrow? Sacrifice money for happiness in the workplace—or can I even find happiness in the workplace? Maybe I should just go for money and buy happiness in my personal time. I think that our generation as a whole is more educated on the long-term impacts of decisions and we feel that burden bearing down on us. *We must make the right decisions,* or else. Or else what? We may end up at age 40 hating our job and lives and wondering where the time went."

Baby boomers often tell their children how lucky they are to have so many more opportunities than there were thirty years ago (along the lines of "When I was your age, I had to walk seven miles to work. In heavy snow. With no feet"). But this increasingly long list of choices actually makes it *harder* to be a twentysomething. With so many more alternatives available, it is more difficult to decide on one particular path. For Olivia, a 22-year-old in Raleigh, North Carolina, the proliferation of opportunities for her career, geographic location, and studies makes it more difficult for her to settle any one aspect of her life. There's just too much going on in her head. "Some people feel anxious after graduation because they can't think of anything they want to do. If anything, I'm anxious because there are so many things I would like to do," Olivia says. "I'm sure I'm not even qualified for half the things I think up, and I bet I won't get some of the jobs that really interest me. Still, I am concerned about having a very full life: being able to do all that interests me, and travel all over the world. I am afraid that I might get locked into whatever job and location I pick now, right after graduation. That is why I am determined to move far away from home in my first year in the real world. I wouldn't mind settling down and raising a family, but I am afraid that if I settle in one place now, I may never leave. I guess my other major concern is that at some point I will have to make a decision whether or not I want to pursue an academic career. I just hate the idea that I will have to move to wherever I can get a job (as is often the case for academics). Or, I might spend ten years getting a Ph.D. and then find I can't get a teaching position anywhere. I can't decide."

It is important to remember that, while it might seem to twenty-somethings that every adult decision they make is entirely their decision, that may not always be the case. "I always have to wonder: where is the person who decides what they really think apart from the influence of family, friends, and the culture in which he finds himself? Who has made even a single decision where the only factor was self-interest? And why on earth would anyone want to?" asks Andrea, a 22-year-old graduate of Sarah Lawrence College (Bronxville, New York). She says that the prevalent turn-of-the-century attitude that people make decisions alone is misleading; it recalls the "me generation" of the 1980s and suggests that recent graduates live in insulated bubbles apart from all of the influences they have ever known in their lives, which is a false notion. "Even more absurd is the fact that the very people who espouse these beliefs are, themselves, espousing the dominant moral code of the day. Their emphasis on the individual, coupled with their insistence on using 'true for me/true for you' language, absolutely *reeks* of this particular time in history, and this particular culture."

Andrea's point is both reassuring and disheartening. On one hand, twentysomethings feel that, as independent adults, they finally have the freedom to be making their own decisions, and yet at the same time, they don't have to make their choices alone. On the other hand, she suggests that society encourages individualistic thinking but also puts constraints on young people so that it is more difficult for them to operate on their own.

Moving Right Along

One of the biggest decisions a twentysomething can face is when and where to move. In fact, whether or not to move can be one of the first major decisions a recent graduate has to make after college, which makes it an even more complex decision. "We're so used to every four months having new classes, every year living somewhere different; and now things get boring when you're two years out and you've been in the same place for too long," says Amanda, a 24-year-old from Little Rock, Arkansas. "I think it was good that I moved where I didn't know a lot of people, just because it forced me to go through some hard times. I know other people who just hang out with their college friends; it's safe and you're not particularly forced to stretch as much. Now I can't decide if I want to move again, but it's not like all of my problems would disappear if I move. And if I move to a new city now, it would be easier because I feel better about myself and know better ways to do things. There's something that I can't feel, that I'm searching for, that would be wherever I live, I think."

Marnel, a 28-year-old from Honolulu, still wonders if he made the right choice by relocating to the East Coast. "The culture on the East Coast is very different from the culture in Hawaii," he says. "Hawaii is more laid back, while everything is fast-paced here—even the little things that you wouldn't suspect, like the fact that everyone walks really quickly in the East. There are no beaches here like there are in Hawaii, where the physical beauty just stands out. At home, you spend the day outside surfing, while here you go to a movie, or museum, or bookstore. It would be nice to go back." But at the same time, he adds, "The social scene in Hawaii for single young professionals is not as good. And while in either place you can seek out activities, it's easier to find nightlife here."

It takes courage and determination not only for twentysomethings to move to a new city, but also to make it once they get there. Moving somewhere new requires starting from scratch, which is scary. But almost all of the twentysomethings who told us about their decisions to move somewhere new said that, although they went through some difficult times, they never regretted moving. "I debated moving to a large city after college for some time. It seemed everything was against me: not having the money to move here, not being able to find a job that would pay enough, not knowing where to live or who to live with. Plus, my father thought it was a bad decision," says Jen, a 1997 graduate of Duke University (Durham, North Carolina). "But despite the obstacles, I made it happen. Do I regret moving alone to a new city? No. Has it been hard? Most definitely. Moving somewhere alone is an incredible growth experience. I have become more independent and have found that I can handle so many things on my own. I have had to deal with incredibly lonely times. Having to manage so many levels of emotions and just normal day-to-day life problems while living on my

How Do I Know If the Decisions I'm Making
Are the Right Ones?

own, away from loved ones, has made me stronger and wiser, and it has taught me things about myself and my limits as well as my goals."

Stacy, a 23-year-old in Arlington, Virginia, says that moving to a city where she didn't know a single person was one of the best decisions she ever made. "The sense of independence and freedom I have from making such a decision is immeasurable," she says. "After graduation I thought a lot about moving to Chicago, where I grew up. My family no longer resides there, so I wouldn't have been moving back home, at least in a traditional sense. But even though my family had gone (and most of my friends, too), and I would have been living downtown, where I spent very little time growing up, I realized after some time that I was just trying to move back home. I longed for that familiarity. So I made a choice to move out of my realm of comfort. I am so glad I did. By moving here I have grown in ways that would not have been possible had I just moved back 'home.'"

One tough choice can be whether or not to move away from everything that is familiar to a twentysomething: a hometown, family, childhood friends. But another choice can be whether or not to move back. "Since graduating from college three years ago, I've experienced an overwhelming period of introspection and change," says Claudia, a 1997 graduate of St. Lawrence University (Canton, New York). After graduation, she found a job in a major city near her university. The city was teeming with young professionals and a hot night life, and Claudia's college friends lived only minutes away. She expected that she would be unquestionably, deliriously happy. Instead, she says, "I found myself unhappy and confused. It took me about a year to realize that my job did not fulfill me as I originally thought it would, I couldn't see my friends as much as I wanted, and the weather prevented me from enjoying my hobbies and interests. It took even more time before I mustered up the courage to pick up my life and move on. It was one of the most difficult decisions I've had to make, and was even harder to follow through with. I decided to move back to my hometown, where my parents reside. Many of my friends thought I was crazy to just quit my job, leave my friends, and move back to my hometown. What they didn't grasp was that on summer vacations during college, while they went home every summer to their parents' homes and worked fun part-time jobs, I lived on my own in a major city working a full-time job. So I tasted true independence and life on my own in the real world before graduation. As I made my decision to move, I realized that life is short, work is just work, and relationships with family and friends are to be cherished in this lifetime. I wanted to move back to my hometown to spend time as an adult with my parents, who sacrificed so much to improve my life."

Claudia says she has not regretted her decision to move back home, for several reasons. Because she was between jobs, she figured she may as well study for the GMAT—she knew she would want to go to business school at some point. When her friends told her she was spending more time studying than they were working at their full-time jobs, she explained that she found it easy to find motivation because she was doing something that she had set out to do on her own. After the boards, she spent a few months traveling and then found a job within a few weeks. She got an apartment that was fairly equidistant to her office, friends, and family. How does she know she made the right decision? "I learned how much strength I had when I moved back home with my parents with no job plans. I assured myself that maintaining faith, setting goals, and keeping an open perspective would allow me to accomplish what I set out to do with my life," Claudia says. "Although I dearly miss my friends from my first job and from college, I know that I made the right decision for myself. Now I frequently talk to friends who dream of moving to new places. The worst mistake you can make is to regret that you didn't try something in the past. I believe your twenties is the time to explore and experiment before settling down. What I learned is that only you can know when the time is right to make a monumental change in your life, whether it is changing jobs, ending a romantic relationship, or moving to a new city. Life is too short to waste on 'If only I . . .' statements. The only way you can figure out who you really are is through the adventures of life and the people you meet. If you silence your passions, you could miss out on a great discovery. There are no mistakes in these decisions. Your life is what you make of it and from these experiences you learn who you really are."

Often, it seems, once twentysomethings make one major decision, like moving, they find other decisions somehow easier to make. Part of this can be attributed to the newfound self-confidence associated with the realization that they can do things entirely on their own, after all. Another factor is that the mere act of picking up and moving will automatically provide a graduate—no matter how recent—with that ever-elusive trait known as "experience," which equips a person with the wisdom to figure out future decisions less stressfully. Carin, a 25-year-old in Long Grove, Illinois, lived at home with her parents in Sweden for six months after she finished school. When she decided they were driving her crazy, she made the transatlantic move to an entirely new country. She wanted something new, and she thought life would be easier because of the little things, like the fact that in the United States, employees generally get paid every other week, while paychecks come only monthly in Sweden. In the United States, she planned to be an au pair and take classes in international marketing. "The first time I moved to the U.S. I was crying because I didn't know if I really wanted to do it—I didn't know if it was the right decision to move in as an au pair with a family I had never seen and never talked to. The family wanted to know where I was at all times, and I had a curfew because I had to use their car. People at home didn't think I was going to make it because I'm Mommy's little girl," she says. "But I changed. I took care of four kids in another country, in another language. When I came home and met with my old friends in Sweden, they were still at the same stage as they had been when I left. So I came back. It gets easier to make the big decisions as you grow; but it helped to know that if I didn't like it in the U.S., I could always go back home. You get used to being away from your parents. I met my fiancé here and we're going back to live in Sweden in a few weeks, but now my fiancé, who is American, thinks I'm the one who is going to want to come back. I might. I've done it before."

How Do I Know If I'm Sure About Somebody?

Carin and her fiancé's decision to move back to Sweden brings up one of the hardest decisions that twentysomethings (and anysomethings, really) feel they have to make, especially for young adults who buy into the old-fashioned theory that they need to meet the person they are going to marry by the time they hit the age of 30. The question that twentysomethings feel more deeply than "When should I marry?" or "When am I ready to settle down?" is the often agonizing debate over whether or not the person whom they think they could marry is the person they really should be with for the rest of their lives.

Wayne, a 1994 graduate of Chipola Junior College (Marianna, Florida), says that twentysomethings frequently put pressure on themselves to be sure about somebody relatively early on in a relationship so that they will have that decision made and therefore won't have to torment themselves with it any longer. "Don't push yourself too soon to be sure about someone else. At times we want to be sure about someone else too soon and don't give everything enough time to just play out," he says.

Twenty-two-year-old Olivia is already trying to figure out how much she should invest in her British boyfriend. If they are to be together long-term, she reasons, it would make sense to compromise at least some of her dreams in order to spend time with him. But if they are not meant to be, then why is she wasting her time? "This is perhaps the most stressful question for me. My boyfriend is moving to Tennessee next year, and I know he wants me to move in with him, but I have little interest in going to Tennessee. At first, this seemed to be a real problem," she says. "Upon reflection, I think it may be a blessing in disguise. We have been dating for over a year, and it is the first serious relationship for the both of us. I have concluded that a year apart may be just what we need to evaluate whether we ought to remain together. Still, I am plagued by doubts. Without me, he might be miserable. But I know that if I just do things to please him, I myself might end up miserable. I might end up really resenting him. I just don't know."

Olivia's dilemma is common among twentysomethings who find a potential partner during or soon after college and then wonder if they should hang onto a good relationship or shop around for a better one. But it is a gamble—they don't know if a better match is out there, and if they look, they might lose what they have already. At the same time, the early twenties are often a time when people want the freedom to do whatever they need to do to figure themselves out, which is more difficult when they also have to consider the needs and feelings of a significant other. Moreover, the twenties are supposedly a time to start experiencing the world of adult dating, which many recent graduates want to experience as fully as they can before they eventually settle down. Once they reach the ages of 26 or 27, however, many twentysomethings told us that their outlooks change. Suddenly, because they are closer to 30 than they are to 20, they feel that dating for the sake of dating is a waste of time that could be spent searching seriously for a spouse. They want to know early on in a relationship whether or not it could work for the long haul, because if not, then they shouldn't bother. Often, twentysomethings wish they could believe in the one concept that would untangle all of these romantic messes for them. If there is indeed such a thing as love at first sight, then they will know where a relationship stands or where it doesn't. They wish they could believe in the idea, but at the same time they may believe that it is a cop-out.

For twentysomethings, the idea of love at first sight meets with reactions ranging from skepticism to hope, but most of the people with whom we spoke said that the idea is basically a myth. They think that the only times people seem to buy into that theory is when they are already married—and then they gloss over their rocky romantic history with their partners and claim they really knew all along. As a result, many twentysomethings worry that if they were to rely on the media-engendered notion that someday they will meet someone and be struck by a mental (and groinal) bolt of lightning, then they will essentially be waiting forever for a feeling that will never happen. "Tough one," says Rick, a 25-year-old in New York City. "I'm not sure if you're referring to a soulmate, but I will assume you are. I like to think that you will just know someday. That it'll be magic, blah, blah, blah. That's nice if the whole 'We fell in love at first sight' thing works out for you, but I think it doesn't happen to most people. I think most people arrive at a point in a relationship where it just makes sense to stay together or not, and where you both have the same idea of the 'importance' of marriage. And women who want to have kids are also an issue and a time bomb. Men have the luxury, the dream of plucking a fertile 24-year-old when they are 30-plus. Like I said, it's a tough question. I'm still working on it myself."

Because they don't want to hold out for some unlikely form of divine intervention, twentysomethings eventually let their attitudes toward love evolve as they gain more romantic experience. Victoria, a 25-year-old New Yorker, says that she has come to believe that she has to know herself thoroughly before she will be ready to know what kind of person will serve as a good complement. "First, know thyself. How can a person make a decision about something if they are uncertain how they will be affected?" she says. "I've learned that people make decisions based upon what is right for them at that particular point in their lives. I think it's foolish to decide on something and believe it will be the right choice always. These kids who are getting married at 21 and 22 years old scare me to death. How can you know yourself fully at such a young age? How can you be certain that your life partner will be right for you ten years down the road? People change. Their needs change as well. I always ask people who are getting married or are already married, 'How did you know this was the right person for you?' The universal response is 'I just knew.' I've been in love a few times and thought those people were the right ones. I'm not sure if I'll ever 'just know.' This is an area of life that I'm still trying to figure out. So when I'm 65 and getting hitched for the first time, you'll know that I've finally figured it all out."

Doug, a 27-year-old graduate of the University of Iowa (Iowa City), says he has learned to apply the decision-making tactics he uses in the rest of his life to his choices in romantic relationships. "One of the big things I've had to get over since college—that I guess I'm still getting over—is the idea that there's always one right answer for everything. I spent a large part of my time in engineering classes in school, and they emphasized (and even many of my social science classes pushed the notion) that there must be one right answer. But in the real world, that's never true. It's not true in politics, on the job, or even in relationships. I've found that even in my career, every single day we have to make the best decisions based on the information we have, and then we move on. If we make mistakes, then we figure out how to fix them and move on. Of course, this is all especially true in social situations, and in romantic relationships. I believe that you can't depend on finding the 'perfect' person or the perfect relationship; you just have to find one that is really, really good and that will withstand the test of time. You have to be mature enough to realize that mistakes will be made but that you can fix them and move on. And you have to be willing to put yourself on the line—to risk making those mistakes—in order to reap the benefits of the good decisions."

Russ, a 25-year-old living in Boston, explained at length why decision making can be so difficult for twentysomethings in the twenty-first century—and what they can do to make this period easier. While he agrees that life is not a series of cut-and-dried mathematical problems, he suggests that recent graduates can view it as a test—a perspective that can ease the transition from college to the rest of their lives:

"I think decision-making is one of the biggest challenges people our age face today, and because everything we do in life requires a decision of some kind, it's a vitally important skill to master. The only problem is, knowing which decisions are wise and which are foolish or imprudent isn't always clear-cut. Even when we can distinguish between a sensible and not-so-sensible choice, we don't always have the discipline to follow our heads. The fundamental decisions we must make in our lives are the very same ones faced by our parents and their parents and their parents; really they are the same questions that humans throughout history have asked themselves. What to do for a living? Whom to choose as a spouse? What to spend money on? What to do in our free time? Where to live? How large a family to raise? With this repository of experience available to us, whether through our parents, grandparents, or other 'grown-up' friends, we should have plenty of guidance in how to approach the big life issues.

"But we really don't. People of our generation have so many more factors and choices to consider in answering these questions than any previous generation—even our parents'. Just compare the choices available to us for careers, spending money, and traveling with those available to people our age thirty years ago. So while we're asking the same questions as, say, the ancient Egyptians, our list of potential answers is much, much longer.

How Do I Know If the Decisions I'm Making
Are the Right Ones?

"At first, this may seem like a raw deal—like we've reached the million-dollar question and our lifeline friend on the phone can't help us one bit. But viewed another way, it gives us extraordinary power in choosing our own destiny. Unlike so many people in ages past (and even today in some parts of the world), we are not limited by outside forces in our choice of career, spouse, place of residence, or ability to purchase things. Essentially, the only limits we have are the ones we place (or allow to be placed) on ourselves. We can still seek the advice of our elders, but the experiences they can share with us will only be a partial help.

"How we respond to these essential (existential?) questions of life largely defines who we are. Years from now, we will look back with pride on the noble decisions we made and look back with regret or embarrassment on our less-than-finest hours. So decision making is important in the present, but its greatest ramifications may not come to light until years in the future. This poses a problem in that with each passing year, it becomes more and more difficult to reverse or alter our prior decisions and actions. If we make a bad decision at age 22, it may affect us throughout our entire life. Of course, we don't want to burden ourselves with unnecessary pressures when making decisions. So how can we approach decision making with appropriate seriousness, but without blowing the potential results and ramifications out of proportion? And how can we determine whether we're on the right track without causing panic and stress if we discover that we're not?

"The way I approach these questions is essentially to treat all of life like an open-book essay exam. The answers are never clear-cut and you don't get your grade back for an eternity—when you do, the comments are often cryptic anyway—yet you have plenty of places to turn for assistance.

Despite the way decisions are often presented in life, it is not a multiple-choice or true-or-false test. We are frequently called upon to explain and rationalize our decisions in life, and even if not required to by others, we ought to be doing it for ourselves. Occasionally, we may be presented with second chances—a retest, if you will—and that's a key reason why self-evaluation is so important. When we find ourselves with a second chance at something, whether it's a personal relationship or a career move, we have no excuse not to seize it.

"When I'm evaluating a 'day-to-day life decision' I've made, like going out on a Saturday night rather than studying for an upcoming professional exam, the first thing I consider is whether I was being honest with myself during the decision-making process. Since I'll never be able to improve my decision-making skills if I don't follow through with what I know is the right course of action, I need to separate the decision I reach in my mind from the one that I actually act out. In the case of staying in and studying versus going out with friends, I may say, 'I won't get much studying done tonight anyway, so I might as well go out and let some steam off' when I know that I desperately need the extra hours of preparation. My decision to go out was really a decision to stay in that I didn't have the self-discipline to carry out. Often, in day-to-day decision making, misguided decisions are not as much of a problem as insufficient self-discipline. While day-to-day decision making is a minor part of our lives when we look at the big picture, it can have an important conditioning effect on how we deal with more weighty issues. If we make wise choices in the ordinary structure of our days and weeks, we will likely have more time, money, and energy to plan bigger and better things, like vacations and big-ticket

How Do I Know If the Decisions I'm Making
Are the Right Ones?

purchases, for instance. We'll also be better prepared to sensibly evaluate the larger life decisions that arise, like choosing or changing careers, finding a spouse, buying a house, planning a family, etc.

"Ultimately, we are all responsible for ourselves and our actions, however major or minor they seem. We must bear the consequences of our decisions, even if we now recognize that some of them were misguided. Each of us has a highly individualized system for decision making, comprised of personal experience, advice from others, common sense, and gut feeling, and the best we can do is refine that system based on lessons learned from our own past choices. If you want to continue having fun in life, don't stop; this is completely normal. If you do desire to stop having fun and enjoying life, you should get a job at your local DMV—it's a great place to make lots of other people miserable (especially fragile teenagers). But there is more to life than having fun or making other people miserable. Life is a test and tests are not supposed to be easy. If they were, there'd be little satisfaction in doing well on them. The greatest joys we find in life almost always come from the toughest trials. But like other tests, if you keep a positive outlook, pay attention to what's going on around you, and take the time to analyze your mistakes, you'll have nothing to worry about."

Natasha, a 1996 graduate of Prince George's Community College (Largo, Maryland), says she simplifies romantic relationships down to one basic premise: gut instinct. "Learn to rely upon this, because it's the only way you know you're making decisions that will make *you* truly happy. Remember that fighting is not fun and should be avoided in a relationship. This doesn't mean conflict and confrontation is bad— just fighting. If you can fight with someone and say, 'I may not like you right now, but I still love you,' that's a good indicator that you're sure about somebody. Then there comes a point where you're never really sure, but you have to try sometime, because otherwise life will pass you by."

Gut Instinct

Despite their misgivings about the idea of some sort of romantic intuition, many twentysomethings told us that there is something to be said for the idea of acting on gut instinct. Whether they are trying to decide on a job, a location, or a living arrangement, sometimes, they say, you really do just know. Keith, who in 1998 earned a master's degree in deaf education from Gallaudet University (Washington, D.C.), says he has made his life decisions based on his instinct that he would always want to work with the deaf. "As long as I can remember, I have wanted to teach the deaf. It was a calling, just like a priest or any other calling. It is not that I felt pity or sympathy. It is just that I knew this is what I should do. I am passionate about it. When I did get my first job in the field, I cried tears of joy. This is something that I had been working toward. It was not Wimbledon or an NBA championship, but it was a goal that I've had for my whole life," he says. "Now that I have been teaching for two years, I know I was right. It is a field that I have given my heart and my soul to. I feel alive when teaching. I can communicate and teach deaf children and bring them equal to and beyond their hearing peers. It is a feeling of elation when I have taught something and the student has understood."

Tara, a 1994 graduate of Clark University (Worcester, Massachusetts), relied on gut instinct for her decisions both to follow her dream job and then to get out of it. "Sometimes the choices that seem most automatic or convenient are the right ones, because you make them based on gut instinct," she says. "I had never really thought of pursuing dance professionally, but after college, I reasoned that I had no real pull toward another direction, and, more to the point, I had been dancing in college, I had connections in New York, and I was young. So I took random jobs—tutoring, waiting tables, baby-sitting, teaching for the Princeton Review, catering—and auditioned, took classes, taught yoga, and performed. I met people whom I will always treasure, I had a crazy and wonderful few years, and I had my time as a performer, living in that insane, difficult, educational, and rewarding world."

After four years of dancing, Tara had an epiphany that led to her swift decision not to dance anymore. So she followed her instinct and moved on with her life. "On vacation after an exhausting performance period, I suddenly realized I didn't want to go back to more auditions, more rejections, more two A.M. nights with sore feet and a bruised ego. I had gotten what I was going to get out of it, and it didn't feel right to push farther. I didn't have that kind of drive toward 'dance and only dance' that one needs to make a career out of it," she says. "I began thinking about the next stage, which I always had known would come. I just didn't realize how the transition would be. I thought it out, didn't rush, stayed in New York while I looked into graduate programs and opportunities overseas, and generally tried to shape this vague desire to move on into something more concrete. It's an ongoing process of discovery that I have realized will always be evolving. There will always be something new to try; there will always be realizations that what you're doing at a particular time will not be the perfect fit forever. Though that's unsettling, it keeps you awake. It's been two years since that first epiphany, and I'm off to grad school in the fall, having worked overseas and moved cities for a job in the U.S. Change is horrifying and full of doubt, but any other way and you're just stuck."

Lauren, a 1996 graduate of Northwestern University (Evanston, Illinois), says her intuition tells her not only that a tough decision that she made has turned out okay, but also that she will continue to be okay when she has to make more tough decisions in the future. "This could also be something I learned in college but did not realize until just this moment. My years at school were (as for most people) my first time away from my family, friends, and all that was familiar. Through all of my experiences, I always knew that I had a home I could return to if things got rough, but I knew there was a great big world out there that I needed to experience. After leaving school I knew that I didn't want to move back to my small town of eight hundred people, because there was limited opportunity. I moved to another large city on my own, but I had a few friends from college that I knew here," she says. "After three years, all of those original friends have left, but I have made new friends. I miss my family dearly, and it is tough to be away when they get together for birthdays or picnics, but something inside me tells me that I am in the right place and that eventually it will all make sense."

Gray Matter

Some twentysomethings try to ease the stress of decision-making by reminding themselves that life is not mathematics; there is no one right answer. Instead of black-or-white, right-or-wrong choices, the plethora of alternatives out there generally fall into a hazy gray area. At the same time, it also might not be realistic anymore for twentysomethings to believe that one thing—one job, one home, one romantic partner— will reach the flawless ideal they envisioned as children.

"There seem to be so many choices out there for what to do, where to go, what to give your life's energy away to. At the same time, there is a total void of situations that would fit me perfectly," says Gabriella, a 1996 graduate of Oberlin College (Ohio). "How to do something I love and survive financially? How to find those things that I love to do that I won't get tired of? I think it might be more like the situation chooses me—sometimes trying too hard ruins everything. I guess I don't approach my decisions thinking that one path is right and the other is wrong, though. To choose to travel to a destination, to take a certain job, to even go to see a movie or see a certain friend—these all could bring consequences, links, and adventures. Nothing is black or white, positive or negative; in the end, any way you go, you learn something new or get led in some new direction. I realized this while I was travelling for a few months on my own in Australia and Indonesia. Every day brought about new decisions, people to meet, places to see, topics of conversation. It was amazing to me that when I just relaxed and enjoyed myself and my own company, life worked out. I started to meet incredible people, went to some of the most beautiful places, and learned to put my faith in myself, my intuition, and the things around me. Even my negative experiences, like getting cheated by others, weren't so bad, since they weren't life threatening and I learned from the circumstances. It's not as easy now that I'm home again and have to go to work every day and pay off my debts, but I've retained that relaxed faith in the future."

Dylan, who received a master's degree in 1995 from North Carolina State University (Raleigh), says that twentysomethings need to view decisions as rife with a range of possibilities, rather than as correct or incorrect answers to specific questions. "Act on decisions and adjust as you go," he says. "Assuming that decisions are either 'right' or 'wrong' is not a good idea—decisions are too complex and their costs and benefits change from moment to moment. There are, however, pointers. Try not to overcommit yourself to any single path. No one path will suit you over your entire life, so it is best to keep somewhat flexible. I have known for a long time that I want to be a teacher. I have also known for a long time that I want to be an anthropologist. Keeping those two goal points in mind, I've kept my path toward those goals somewhat flexible. I spent four years getting my B.A., with one of those years spent in England for subject-intensive study, and another four working my way through my M.A. and the coursework for my Ph.D. After completing the coursework, I joined the Army (in part to conduct research necessary for my doctoral dissertation). I spent two and a half years exploring a radically different lifestyle. I learned a lot about myself and discovered that my two great passions of teaching and anthropology remain with me through everything. Maybe some of my decisions weren't perfect, but a positive attitude will carry even the most misguided person through life intact."

Some twentysomethings take Dylan's perspective in a slightly different direction; they say that while it is possible for decisions to be wrong, those mistakes can be helpful. Learning from wrong decisions can ensure better judgement in the future, and besides, as Victoria says, if twentysomethings don't make the decisions in the first place, they will never know which ones are right. "Ten months ago, I decided to get my own apartment. I had had roommates for six years and thought I would try living on my own for a while. I wasn't sure that I knew the entire 'me' and hoped I'd find out if I lived by myself. I decided not to have a television or computer in my apartment—anything that would distract me from my thoughts," she says. "At first I hated it. It was too quiet and I felt really alone. But I started to become introspective and thought about the person I am and the direction I wanted to take in life. It allowed me to obtain answers to questions I didn't even know I had about myself. This was a decision I chose to make on my own, and I'm more self-aware because of it. What if it totally backfired and ended up being the wrong choice? Then I would have dealt with it and moved on. I think it's okay to make the wrong decisions. We can't always know the right path to venture onto, but we'll never know unless we choose one."

Many recent graduates say that instead of debating a decision over and over again, they should just make the decision to make a decision and go with it. Because these years should be fluid, not stagnant, they say, twentysomethings need to take risks, see how their choices turn out, assess them after the fact, and then take it from there. "How do you know if the decisions you're making are the right ones? You don't know and that's it," says Rick, a 25-year-old in New York City. "You have to accept the fact that you can't cut yourself in two and walk different paths. You make choices and, by doing so, give up other opportunities. I think it's more important to be able to make decisions, to take a risk. A friend once told me that you regret what you did not do more than the stuff you did. And I think that best sums up the importance to *make* a decision, be it the 'right' or 'wrong' one."

Going with It

Rick's suggestion seems so simple, but it represents an attitude that many optimistic twentysomethings have toward the multitudes of choices they have to make at this point in their lives. These young adults espouse two beliefs that sustain their healthy attitudes toward this difficult crossroads. First, there will never be a time when all of their decisions have been made, because life is a series of choices that twentysomethings just have to keep on making. And second, the less common view, that somehow, inexplicably, no matter what decisions they make, things end up working out okay in the end.

Twenty-six-year-old Frank says that this mellow attitude has worked for him. Near the end of his second year at college he transferred to Berkeley, where he didn't know anybody, but where more opportunities awaited. He was lonely when he began his junior year at Berkeley, but he quickly stumbled on a job that soon consumed all of his free time. "Never had I imagined I would or could sell cars, but there I was taking a full load at school and putting in forty-plus hours per week at a Ford dealership, schlepping new and used autos. It turned out to be a job at which I excelled," he says. "By the time I graduated, I had set two goals I thought would bring me happiness beyond my most distant horizons. I wanted to be the youngest finance manager in California and I wanted to make $100,000 per year. Within three years I had exceeded both goals, but I found myself, for the first time in my life, unexpectedly lacking focus. In just six months, I went from a driven achiever who owned a house and three cars to an unsettled, obstinate, searching twentysomething. Working sixty to seventy hours per week, weekends, holidays, and evenings finally got the best of me. What had for so long slept in the back of my mind as a distant, unachievable dream suddenly became my highest aspiration. I walked into work one day in September and declared I was quitting. Forty-five days later, escrow closed on my house, all my belongings were packed, and the cars were sold. Since then I have been happily traveling around the globe."

Frank just packed up and left. For twelve months of travel, he budgeted $20,000 (a cap that he expects to exceed by $10,000 because he thinks he might travel for an additional year. Plus he bought a 4X4 in Australia). "Although it would be a lie to claim I harbored no fear when I made the decision to quit, I did it with the conviction and self-assurance that it was the proper decision. How correct I was would not become clear till some months later. Wading into the ninety-five-degree waters of the tropical lagoon in front of my hut on Kadavu Island, Fiji, a full moon and clear sky above, waves crashing on Astrolabe Reef a hundred yards from shore, working became a distant memory. I found paradise to be a cleansing place, particularly as I had no plans to leave. It was then I knew with one hundred-percent assurance that the proper choice had been made. Should I have left sooner? No, had I left earlier, I might now be wondering if I was really disgusted with my job and my industry enough to justify a permanent exit," he says. "As things now stand, I could not be more sure that I never want to work in the car business again. What's more, I am now free to fulfill another dream of attending graduate school, which I could not have done even on a part-time basis before. Quitting a job that disgusts you can almost never be a poor decision. To replace such a job by undertaking protracted international travel was undoubtedly the right choice for me."

Frank didn't know at the time that he was making the right decision. But he made his choice, went with it, and in the process created new opportunities for himself. There is no one answer to the question, "How do I know I'm making the right decisions?" But as the responses of many twentysomethings imply, an acceptable explanation could be, "You don't. But you make them anyway."

six

How Do I Work Out the Right Balance Among My Career, Friends, Family, and Romance?

One of the most important tasks of the twentysomething years is to learn how to maintain a good balance among one's career, friends, family, and romantic life. There is no one ideal for everybody; rather, the way a person chooses to weigh these important aspects is part of what makes him who he is. Discovering the right balance is especially hard because it is also a constantly changing process. Maybe during one's early twenties, focusing on a career could be a person's highest priority, while later on, a new family could take precedence. Or perhaps, just after school, a graduate may concentrate on continuing college friendships so that they don't quickly fade, and cultivating new ones in order to streamline his social network; but after a few months, he finds a girlfriend and many of those friends fall by the wayside. Because these choices are so individual, no one can tell a twentysomething which aspects of life should take precedence at which times.

A good way to look at this struggle is to see a twentysomething as a rookie quarterback. Say this guy has just turned pro. The veteran experiences a season-ending injury in the last preseason game, so the rookie, who has not taken many snaps with the first string or even thoroughly learned the playbook, is now the starter. It's opening day. Big game. The rookie takes the field. Factoring out the coaches and the old QB, who barks commands into his headset, the rookie quarterback's dilemma is, in a way, like a twentysomething's balancing problem: even though he is inexperienced, he has to decide what to emphasize in order to make the best of his situation at this present time. Say he has a star running back, a versatile tight end, and a couple hotshot wide receivers. He has to choose which one to use on this first play.

So what does he do? He analyzes his field position. He reads the defense. He listens to his teammates. But to claim that he will base his decision only on those techniques would be to oversimplify. He also has to factor in the field condition, the condition of his teammates (if the right guard has turf toe, the quarterback might not head that way), and the condition of his opponents (has their run defense been shoddy lately?). But wait; there's more. He has to consider the good relationships he has with his teammates (if he has connected already with a particular receiver, the quarterback may be better able to hit the receiver on his route), and the relationships he has yet to forge (if he alienates the other receiver early, he could have trouble finding him later). In some cases, he might have incentive-based bonuses (completion percentage, rushing yards). He will think about the fans, who will let him know, loudly, what they believe he should do—and how much they dislike his choices. And he will consider where this play will lead—how will it set him up for the next play? Then he will make his decision, prioritize his assets, and run the play. The difference between the quarterback and a regular twentysomething, of course, is that the quarterback has, more often than not, less than a minute to make his decision and go with it, audibles included. (And a nicer car.) But both individuals have a lot of factors to weigh before figuring out what or whom to prioritize, and both individuals, at first, don't have a lot to go on.

Granted, the rookie quarterback isn't going to go through the equivalent of a quarterlife crisis every time he approaches the line of scrimmage. Football may be his career, but it is also only a game. For twentysomethings who don't have the luxury of NFL sponsorship, this conflict has much more far-reaching ramifications. Recent graduates frequently feel like the way they tip the balance now will affect them for years to come. This can contribute to a quarterlife crisis when twentysomethings' balance is out of whack, when they are having a tough time figuring out the right balance, or when they are trying to do the actual balancing. "The hardest part of being a twentysomething is that there is a lot to consider and it's hard to know where to start and how to balance everything," says Joe, who earned a master's degree in 2000 from the University of Pennsylvania (Philadelphia).

Stuff Happens

Another way a quarterlife crisis can occur is when, as happens more often than many twentysomethings anticipate, priorities change when they least expect them to. For Jill, the struggle to balance aspects of her life completely dominated her first two years out of Western Washington University (Bellingham).

"My father always said I should have an immediate goal and a larger, ten-year plan," Jill says. "I graduated college wanting nothing more than the ultimate job for me—teaching art abroad to elementary-aged children and somehow involving dance in that picture. I figured I'd have to build up to that goal, and that would be my big plan." What Jill hadn't anticipated, though, was that she could fulfill her utmost career goal almost immediately. After graduation, she moved to Keflavik, Iceland, where she taught elementary school art classes to children on the NATO base and ballet to Icelandic youth. "See, I fulfilled my ten-year plan in two months," she says. "So then what?"

The challenges Jill met in her job were at first a bit of a jolt. A young, gung-ho teacher at the bottom of the totem pole, she was initially startled by workplace politics and protocol. The job she had thought would be so exciting turned out to be more drudgery than reward. "I was all excited about the classroom being my 'canvas' and the students being these wonderful, pure creations I could nurture," she continues. "Yeah, okay, so what I learned was that really all I got to focus on was behavior management—as in did little Susie share her crayons with Raymond, and did little Joey sneak out of class to go play at the water fountain." To make matters worse, Jill wasn't able to muster up much of a social life among her older colleagues. There were a few teachers under 30, but most of them, Jill says, "pretty much were into Tupperware and cats."

At the same time, she gradually grew disenchanted with the idea of living in Iceland, which wasn't what she had envisioned. Stuck feeling like she had little in common with her colleagues, and caught in a job that wasn't thrilling, Jill realized that she wouldn't be able to hack five years in Iceland after all. She knew she wanted to find a place and a job that she could be more passionate about, but she had no idea what that would be. The biggest jolt of all, however, was that at a time when she had doggedly prioritized her career categorically above everything else, something unexpected got in the way. When Jill met Rob, a Navy officer, everything changed. Given the summer-camp atmosphere, the few daylight hours, and the serendipity of finding such a strong connection in a small community, Jill and Rob grew close more quickly than they had expected. Part of it was that they were living abroad, but another part of it was that their relationship made the other aspects of their lives seem more bearable.

Rob was relocated by December. Back in Keflavik, Jill tried to tip the balance toward her career. She cultivated her friendships on the island and distracted herself with large projects at school. At the end of the year, after six months of a long-distance relationship, it was time to reassess her balance. This would have been a pretty easy decision to make, had the love of Jill's life not been transferred to South Dakota. (Note to South Dakotans: certain opinions expressed by the twentysomethings in this book do not necessarily represent the views of the authors. Besides, we've never even been to South Dakota. And Jill changes her mind, anyway. Oooh, foreshadowing.)

"South Dakota was not some easy place to pick up and move to, like New York or Seattle or some other well-known cultural hotbed. No, South Dakota was a land I could only foresee as riddled with farms and bake sales," Jill says. She interviewed for a job in Santa Fe, which was in the same time zone (not to mention continent), but seemed to be a more interesting place. Then she realized she wouldn't be moving toward anything in Santa Fe; she would simply be moving. For several weeks, Jill says she was in emotional turmoil. When her parents visited Iceland in June, her father asked her, "So what is your new plan?"

"And suddenly," Jill says, "I didn't have one. All I had was my heart saying I wanted to be with Rob. So I told my father this. He didn't freak out. He actually was pleased to hear that I was interested in setting up some potential roots. So he said he would support me emotionally and even financially if I needed help. With his support I was able to take the huge plunge." In South Dakota, Jill found jobs teaching art at a public school and teaching dance at a private studio. After a few months, though, she changed directions again—she felt more confident because, for the first time as an adult, her personal life was fulfilling. Six months after leaving Iceland, Jill began taking advanced dance classes after she finished teaching. Then she began performing.

Today, Jill's happiness in her personal life and her activities makes her day job fly because she approaches every day looking forward to her dance class, and then coming home to her boyfriend. Through her dance classes, Jill has met other twentysomethings. At the time of this writing (by the time you read this far, who knows what will have changed?), Jill's balance tips unquestionably in favor of her social life and her romantic relationship. People still question the ways that Jill has chosen to balance her life. They still tell her she is giving up on her dreams in order to be with "some guy out in the middle of nowhere." But, she says, "My dream was what happened those first two months out of college. The rest isn't dreams—it's all life. Does it really matter so much if I don't love my day job if everything else is just oozing happiness? It isn't easy to take plunge after plunge, and it's not as clear a plan as it was in college. I feel like I turned a page to live together with Rob. But without him, I wouldn't be here today. I proved to myself that what really matters most for my happiness is to follow my heart, no matter how crazy it sounds, and trust that everything will work out."

Work Won't Make You Coffee in the Morning

Zooming back out to the big picture, Jill's story is clearly a pretty happy one—so happy, at times, you may want to hurl. But it took her a long time to figure out what kind of balance in her life would make her that happy. And she still doesn't know how to upgrade her career so that it will be at least half as satisfying as her personal relationships. She does, however, represent a great many twentysomethings who, despite the lucrative field of dot coms, the favorable job market, and the abounding opportunities to start companies from scratch, are getting greater personal satisfaction from prioritizing relationships above their careers.

Dylan, a 29-year-old who, in 2002, will receive his Ph.D. from North Carolina State University (Raleigh), offers a plausible reason why de-emphasizing a career can keep a twentysomething more grounded. "The only real danger I foresee is if you prioritize your career too much," he says. "Money won't keep you company when you want to share a sunset. It won't laugh with you at life's follies and it won't invite you over for a beer when life is getting you down. If you keep your interpersonal relationships healthy, your career will blossom on its own. If you fail to keep your interpersonal relationships healthy, your work performance will grow uninspired and erratic. Never be afraid to put people above work. Remind yourself what the whole point of a career is—to enable you to live a quality life with friends and family. If you cannot be there for your friends and family, your career is a waste of your energy and time."

This outlook seems to be a pretty popular one among twentysomethings. Take Paula, a 25-year-old from Redmond, Washington. Paula's job requires a lot of travel and some long hours during particular periods of the year. At first, these time and energy constraints were okay for the self-professed workaholic. But then she realized something had to give. "Throughout my whole life, at whatever I did, I was always a hard worker," she says. "I really believed that to get somewhere and make a lot of money, you had to work extra hard. At first I was fine with working long hours. However, as I saw my friends going out all the time or just hanging out, I began to realize that I was missing out both on life and on strengthening my friendships. Sure, my job is important to me, but my young, carefree, single life wasn't going to be around forever, so if I was going to have fun, now was the time to do it. Work would always be work, and I was sure there was nothing important that I would miss out on if I worked fewer hours. Besides, work won't always be there with you the rest of your life, but your friends sure will."

It isn't always that easy to give up career dreams for a posse, or even for a family. Mario, a 27-year-old in Washington, D.C., is in the midst of this struggle. His life is good and his job is good, but the majority of his family and friends happen to live in Massachusetts. The question of how to balance his life, he says, has plagued him since his senior year of college. At first, he debated whether or not to sell his soul to the never-see-daylight world of investment banking. Eventually he took a job in boutique consulting instead. "At this point I am happy with my job and happy enough with my life," he says. "I do, however, feel that I have given up future opportunities by not doing investment banking and that I am missing out on my family, especially my two young nephews. I plan on moving back to Massachusetts to be closer to my family, but only for the right job. Right now I feel that every job that I have determines the next job that I can get. By considering only top-level work I will put myself in a position so that companies all over the country will want me to work for them. That being said, a company near family and friends will have an advantage."

A career may weigh down a social life, but it can also enhance one. Not all jobs take time and energy away from personal relationships—just ask the people who are working alongside their friends, continuing the lineage of a family business, or dating their colleagues (that one is a different book entirely). Some twentysomethings talk about confidants they have developed through their jobs. And some mention the ways their careers drove them to spark changes in the rest of their lives. Twenty-four-year-old Devon's "teacher persona" was a far cry from her usual wild-child self, which caused problems for her outside the work place. "I was having real issues," she says. "I kind of had to be on my 'best behavior,' so to speak, wherever I went, because I would bump into students and parents everywhere. I had to be really aware of silly things, like buying condoms at the grocery store, because the person at the register could be a student. I had to watch my conversations at restaurants, just in case. All of this was really making me a bit paranoid."

After a while, Devon says she realized she was sacrificing too much of herself socially because of her job. Her commute to school was a breeze, but she had to tone down her personality whenever she was in her community—which was often, given that her community encompassed both her work and her home. So her first step was to move a few towns over, where the commute to work wasn't too terrible, but where she was far enough away from school that she wouldn't have to worry about running into her students as she picked through the lingerie store. In her new town, she has befriended a few people at her gym. And, just a few blocks from her apartment, she found a local hole-in-the-wall bar where she has become such a regular that the bartender named a drink after her.

Devon's second step is to try to turn her workplace into a social life. "At first," she says, "it's tough. After college, you're no longer surrounded by people your age to go out and party with. I'm trying at work, but the truth is that most of my colleagues are at least five years older than me and mostly married. But I've found that with some prodding, even a few of the old fuddy-duddy ones will come out for a beer. I try to organize happy hours and stuff. Sometimes it works. Every year I figure they'll hire a few more young guys like myself and I'll just keep trying." Amanda, a 24-year-old from Little Rock, Arkansas, has also tried to improve her social life by mixing work and pleasure rather than viewing them as separate entities. "For the first couple months, I did nothing at work and then I would just come home. I didn't know anyone and I didn't know what to do with my time. It was so different from college because at school we just studied, met with clubs, or went to the gym—we had more organized activities," she says. "I tried to meet people by going to singles events, which was a bust. But then slowly I started to become friends with some of my coworkers. It's better now, even though I've never gotten into the happy-hour thing."

A job can also drive recent graduates to cram the other parts of their lives into their non-working hours. "I suddenly feel like, since I'm working from seven A.M. till eight P.M., I don't have time to do anything. How can I have a life?" asks Ashley, a 1997 graduate of Brown University (Providence, Rhode Island). "And that's not even long hours compared to stock brokerages and places like that. I'm trying to do things outside of work. I've been trying to work out during lunch so I don't feel like my job has so much control over me." While sometimes this can seem exhausting, it can also force people to make sure their lives are balanced. It's kind of like that weird phenomenon in high school: the kid who was a three-sport athlete, played the oboe in the school band, and ran the student government, while volunteering seven days a week at the local soup kitchen (which he founded and named after Mabel, the woman he visited regularly at the old folks' home every Thursday for breakfast and checkers), was inevitably the one who also had the enviably stellar grades. Maybe it wasn't necessarily all that weird. What happened was that the students who had several activities to juggle were invariably the ones who developed the best time-management skills. They had to.

Well, the same thing can happen in the real world. Some recent graduates say they are better able to balance the rest of their lives because their jobs force them to. Because of this situation, Jackie, who graduated in 1999 from Texas A&M University (College Station), says that finding the right balance among her career, friends, and family is the one aspect of her life that she is sure she is handling correctly. "I'm definitely not an expert on the real world yet, but I have had a hell of a year. As a single twentysomething, I am in the luxurious position of not being tied down. I have the ability to be selfish without it negatively affecting others," she says. "Because I often work long days, my social life is a top priority. I'm young enough that I'm not looking for my lifelong mate, which allows me to go out, have fun with my friends, and meet a lot of people. Yet, I'm old enough that I have the confidence, education, and cash to enjoy the atmosphere and company around me without worrying about the irrelevant, stressful details of some party or bar that plagued me in high school and college."

Granted, things shift. This past year, Jackie's mother passed away, which has made her family an enormous priority. Because her weekdays are packed tightly with work and going out with friends, she uses her weekends to spend time with her family and "have 'me' time." And romance? It's the one factor that's missing, Jackie says, but that's okay with her. Contrary to popular belief, romance is not necessarily a hot concern for people who have recently graduated from college. Whether it is because the fling-after-fling habit in college got tiresome, the opportunity to jumpstart a career is too tempting to refuse, or

And then there is the woman thing. Not every topic resonates noticeably differently with male and female twentysomethings. But this one does. When we asked the question in this chapter's title to women, their responses were along the lines of 26-year-old Santa Maria, California native Natasha. "How do I work out the right balance among my career, friends, family, and romance?" Natasha gave us a one-line answer: "Very carefully. This involves a great deal of crying and heartache if you're female."

Emily, a 2000 graduate of the University of Southern California (Los Angeles), articulated this problem best:

"I was writing a script about a Wall Street woman who was suddenly forced to take care of an adolescent boy. The conflict had to do with her career, which she loved and worked hard for, and a person who needed her and whom she also needed. My professor, a 30-year-old single man, nodded and said, 'You're pretty much done. You just need to come up with a clever way that she can have her career and her family at the same time. Moving on...' And I thought, if that answer came that easily, I would be the richest woman in the world for knowing it and women in general would heave a collective sigh of relief.

"Finally, I had to change the nature of the script because I wouldn't allow myself to have her pick either family or career. I had asked a question that I could not answer, and I refused to insult myself and my gender by giving a trite and ridiculous response. I don't think there is an answer to this question, specifically about women and career versus family. When we have children, our bodies naturally love and want to nurture. But in today's age of women kicking ass and taking names in the workplace, we have a chance of doing whatever we want for ourselves. Fundamentally, every day women fight two different natures and two different needs.

"A basketball player at Bowdoin was revered for taking on his baby daughter after his girlfriend left them. He worked, saved, raised a child, went to school, and played a good game. He was on the news with Katie Couric, who interviewed him about his choice. He talked to administrators at the college about his dilemma—barely having enough money to feed his daughter and himself—and received more financial aid. The story was touching and sweet. I turned to my mother and said, 'That is so impressive. Isn't that amazing? Imagine that, him taking his daughter while still in school—and playing *basketball* no less.' My mother stared straight ahead. She said, 'I wouldn't know, since I only raised two young children and got my Ph.D. at the same time.' I realized that my mother, like many, many women, went to school, and raised children, and worked.

"A lot of single women raise their kids while working and training and, for some reason, are never made into a news story. For men, work and career were always their 'job' in life. Family was their support, an extracurricular advantage and reward. For women, family is our designated job. Any career outside that is considered our choice, our extracurricular reward. Something we do on our own time. We feel strongly about both jobs and don't want to give up either—and shouldn't have to—and yet we always get caught having to choose and trying to make everything balance. We are the modern juggler, responsible for producing the next generation of fine citizens as well as finding our own place and our own career.

"For me, I still have no answer to this problem. I badly want a great career. I want to put my soul into my writing and ride out my life still learning my craft. I very, very much want to be a mother. I want to raise a good man, and a good woman. I want to be with my children and cherish them and feel how they affect my life and how I affect theirs. I hate the idea of

> giving in on either side, of accepting a little less just so I can
> have both. My plan is to go full rudder ahead for my career,
> which is an extension of myself, until I fall in love (or don't fall
> in love. I'll have children either way). And then I will see
> where the road takes me. Women must find their own kind of
> balance, giving up some this day and something else the next,
> and ultimately making a day-by-day designer balance that is
> just enough but probably never too much."

something momentous has caused priorities to shift, not every twenty-something is a dripping hormone squeegee desperate to suck in the nearest breathing creature as a soulmate for eternity.

For Elaine, a 24-year-old from Dallas, it has been "virtually impossible" to figure out the right balance. "Family is the only area I have found I can neglect," she says. "Friends are beautiful for giving you a balance between being adored and ignored. Their priorities are real, too. So your relationship with friends, unlike that with your family or a romantic interest, gives you a perspective on people as true individuals." As for romance, Elaine agrees with Jackie. "Romance—ugh. I've never found one that complements all the other important priorities in my life. Especially as a woman, it's difficult to find someone without making some huge sacrifices to your career and friends. Sometimes, I'm so lost about what I want to do that I don't even realize what I'm sacrificing or compromising."

When Love Comes to Town

Elaine says she also leans toward de-emphasizing romance because she sees how her female friends tend to let it take over their lives. When a romantic relationship takes the top spot, it can skew how a twenty-something perceives other priorities. "I'm afraid many of my friends are going to be members of the *Sex in the City* crowd in the next decade," she laments. "Don't misunderstand me. I like the characters, but even their lives seem to revolve around men. They're thirtysomething with exciting and interesting careers, and their Sunday brunches are about their last lay? I'd like to hear just as much about their fabulous clothes. I have been entertained by my romantic trysts. But after my first love betrayed me, I don't think I'm ready for anything that will get in the way of my plans for further education, a career, and travel."

Then again, it is actually possible for a twentysomething to maintain a solid romantic relationship without sacrificing other important things. Jeff, who will graduate in 2003 from Southern Methodist University Law School (Dallas), makes sure he includes as many people in his life as possible, even though his longtime girlfriend usually gets most of his time and attention. "I happen to really value the 'romance' aspect but I've been with the same girl for six years. Everything else is important, too, but not to the same degree. Friends and family play a big part in my life, but not as big as her," Jeff says.

A danger to watch, though, is that friends and family members could quickly and easily feel excluded from a recent graduate's life if he does not make frequent overtures to include them. Jeff goes for the you-can't-please-everybody-but-you-can-try-like-hell technique. "The key is to try to find things to do that make everyone happy," he says. "For instance, my brother and I both love to play soccer. When I made my own soccer team, he was the first person I called. When I join any other team, I ask 'Hey, do you need two extra guys?' instead of 'Do you need another player?' I spend a lot of time hanging out at home with my girlfriend, but if we decide to go out anywhere, then we call up our friends. I don't give everyone equal time, but I try to make sure that I don't make anyone feel that they aren't important to me. As for career, to me, that's secondary. There's nothing more important than personal relationships."

Kim, a 25-year-old from Augusta, Georgia, is still trying to work out how to balance her steady romance with the rest of her life. Up to the point when she met her current, long-term boyfriend, Kim had trouble finding the time and places to meet people and to sustain relationships while she was working long hours at two jobs. "Though I have always been good at maintaining relationships even with people who live far away, I found myself too drained to do so much as call my friends and family. I began to live for the weekends and the brief respite from the long hours of work. I went out virtually every night of every weekend with various friends in the Augusta area, but I found myself in a series of bars, nightclubs, and other venues that do not lend themselves well to conversation and intimacy beyond grinding with strangers on the dance floor. I began to wonder if I would ever be able to hold an adult conversation again," she says.

Now that she has begun dating one person seriously, Kim says she has encountered a new set of problems: balancing her romantic life with her hectic schedule. The lifestyle change, compounded by the fact that her boyfriend lives two hours away, is "enormous" because now she wants to revolve her life around him. "Though this thrills me to epic proportions, it is ludicrously difficult to fit into my schedule. I honestly expected never to love or be loved (though I always hoped I might be wrong) and learned to rely entirely on myself for my own happiness, entertainment, and self-esteem. As a result, not only is it humanly impossible to find time for a man who lives two hours away while working sixty hours a week, but I am also struggling with the conflicting desires of wanting to be with him incessantly and needing to maintain my strength, my edge, my independence, and my ability to take care of myself (thank you very much). Moreover, now that he is in my life, the minimal time I had for friends and family (as well as alone time, and the obnoxious necessities of life like dishes, laundry, cooking, and cleaning) has diminished even further. So, you ask how

I maintain a balance and I reply, I don't, but I muddle through as best I can."

Balancing a social life with a serious romantic relationship can be especially difficult for young married couples, says Jessica, a 1997 University of Pennsylvania graduate who got married at 23. "This has been a real challenge. Most of my friends aren't married, while I have been married for two years. That means I devote a lot of time to my marriage while my other friends are living the single life," she says. "Being married makes socializing more of a challenge than college, where we were all in the same boat. Also, in college, everyone is there for the same purpose: as a student. Now, some of my friends are working, some are in school, and we're all in different cities. So, most of my time during the week is spent at work, and then I spend my weekends traveling around the East Coast to visit friends. And in between I try to see my family—and my husband. But eventually one of these has to take priority. For me, that has been my marriage and my job. But my marriage will always come first."

Many twentysomethings say that they would rather have to balance all of these aspects of life than not have those relationships to balance in the first place. One of the major concerns for twentysomethings who aren't lucky enough to already have a romantic relationship like Jeff's or Jessica's is how to find one. Dan, who lives in Tucson, considers himself pretty well grounded for a twentysomething. Even though he is 24, he says his biggest worries right now are more typical of someone in his late twenties or early thirties. He enjoys his job, but gets stressed sometimes about what he calls his "work/life balance." He says, "I do worry a little bit about the overlap between work and life. When does work end and non-work begin? I'm pretty fortunate—usually I'm done by six-thirty, and I never bring my work home. The only time it gets tough is when I have to travel, because then I have to devote the entire day and night to my job. Although I don't travel much, the fear of having to travel makes me less likely to make a regular commitment."

Dan describes the way he manages to balance his life in terms of a sense of "wholeness." His work is a major part of his identity right now—he says that if he were not happy with his career, he would definitely be unhappy in general—but he has to monitor several facets of his life. "The key to happiness for me is probably a sense of 'wholeness'—making sure I'm taking care of all parts of me. I need to be challenged. I need to be creative. I need to be valued. I need to be loved. And I need time to recharge. I usually don't have all of those things at the same time. I wouldn't know how to prioritize one over the other, so I try to find ways to get them all in. That's why I like my job—because I'm challenged, valued, and very often creative. And it usually leaves me time to recharge. But right now I'm not really being loved."

This missing aspect is one of the most important parts of life for Dan, who, although self-assured, admits he is often anxious about the romance issue. "Really, the only thing I ever wonder about constantly is who the 'right person' for me will be and how I will be able to be a good husband and father—my number one priority—and still manage a thriving, fast-track-ish career, my number two priority." Dan says he has tried to address this part of his life by making an extra effort to find the right woman. He prefers to meet people during organized activities, so he joined an a capella music group and a recreational comedy troupe. He dated a few people he met at parties and one woman who worked at his company, but none of them worked out long-term. "I've tried to meet the right person, but it's difficult," he says. "I probably don't meet enough people to let the odds work for me. I don't usually do well in clubs or places where it's loud because I do best when I can actually have a conversation. I figure I'll meet someone eventually, but not by staying in my apartment." Instead of cutting things out of his life in order to make room for potential girlfriends, Dan says he plans to add elements to his life in the hope that he will meet somebody new. Currently, he is contemplating whether to audition for a musical or do volunteer work.

One effect of all of these balance problems is that they can lead to a lot of stress for twentysomethings, who have never encountered these kinds of challenges before. Because of their lack of experience, young graduates say they doubt their abilities to prioritize properly and their self-esteem falters as they wonder if they will ever be able to fit everything they want into their lives. "I have these important relationships in my life with my family, and leaving them makes you think, 'How important is your career?'" says Maria, a 1996 graduate of Tulane University (New Orleans). "My sister recently had a baby and almost every single person that means the most to me is six hundred miles away. But then again I know that if I was living at home with my family, I would be missing out on my career. And I'm not saying I don't want to be a career woman for the rest of my life, but at the same time I don't have a family right now, so that's what I need to strive for. And that's where my doubts come in: trying to find the balance between striving to accomplish all my goals, set goals, keep going after them, and make my personal life happy."

Because there are no set guidelines for living, Maria says that twentysomethings get lost somewhere in between what they think they should be doing, what society tells them they should be doing, and what they actually want to be doing. "Sometimes I think that I'm four short years away from being 30 and I'm not anywhere close to being married, I'm not anywhere close to having children," she says. "It's just that whole female fear of 'Where am I supposed to be going and how quickly am I supposed to be doing this?' And society has all these parameters set up for women that are so high-pressure. You're supposed to be a mom, and you're supposed to have this successful career. And just getting out of college and having work and going to school full time, I'm realizing that being Superwoman is very exhausting, and I really don't want to do that for the rest of my life. I can't do this forever. I can't live on six hours of sleep for the rest of my life. I don't want to. Sometimes I feel like I need to see a therapist about this, but I know that with time these things will work themselves out."

Carrie, a 1997 graduate of Case Western Reserve University Law School (Cleveland), says that for her the balancing act is frightening because it changes as she changes, and she doesn't have the experience to know how to adapt. For her entire life, she had expected to go to medical school, but when she graduated from college, she wasn't accepted anywhere. "I thought that was what my career had to be, and I really didn't think about whether or not that was what I wanted to do, or what my parents wanted me to do, or what I thought I was supposed to do. And I think I had a lot of learning to do about myself. What's scary is that three years later I still have doubts, and I still feel like I have so much growing to do," she says. "I often say to my friends that I think there are two paths in our twenties that we are very concerned about. One is career and one is falling in love, and I think what it all has to do with is avoiding a feeling of loneliness. A part of me wants to have a path. And I sometimes worry—I think that I've been trying to work really hard the past couple of years on being okay with not having a path, but every time that I would begin to allow myself to feel that, there was a part of me that went, 'You have to have a path.' It's also a lot about feeling trapped. I worry sometimes that I'll never feel like I've arrived, that I'll always have inner turmoil."

The Balancing Act

In this chapter, twentysomethings have discussed the different ways they can balance their lives, the problems they have with the actual balancing, and the difficulties they have with making that balance work for them. But what was harder to get recent graduates to articulate was *how*, exactly, they go about making sure that their friends, family, career, and romantic relationships get the right amount of attention on a daily or weekly basis. Doug, a 1996 graduate of the University of Iowa (Iowa City), offers a specific, surprisingly simple technique to help people realize what is or should be important to them. "You have to make the choices and set the priorities for yourself," he says. "So many people my age—and way too many who are much older than I— have never sat down to even think about what is really important to them and why. They just get up every morning and do their things and go to bed at night. But the trouble is, you wake up one day when you're 50 or 60 and realize that you did have life goals or priorities after all, but you've let other things get in the way. And now it's too late," he says. "I think it's crucial to physically write down personal goals and priorities on a regular basis. Maybe it's every six months, maybe every five years, but goals change and situations change, so you have to do it continually. And the biggest part of the exercise is not to come up with the list, but to understand *why* each goal is on the list and why this priority is higher than that one. You have to challenge yourself. You have to think: 'When I'm 50, am I really going to be happy that I worked out at the gym every single day rather than spent time with my family?' Then, once you have those priorities set, it's so much easier to decide what you want to spend your time on."

To start such a list, it might help to consider the advice of Cathy, a 22-year-old Hunter College (New York City) graduate. She says that twentysomethings should focus on a career because "it will produce the most stability in the future. But," she adds, "you should never neglect any of the other things, or a career is worth nothing." As for the other aspects of living at this age, she offers, "Do not let one of these areas take over, or you will be miserable."

Dylan, the North Carolina State University doctoral candidate, agrees. "A mistake that many people make is that they assume that by prioritizing one aspect of life (say, romance), they have to ignore every other aspect. Or they assume that there is some complex juggling act that must be performed to keep everything going. It is possible to be mindful of one's entire life without having to single out specific elements one at a time." No one is saying that it isn't hard to work out the right weight to place on friends, family, romantic relationships, and a career. But as Dylan suggests, it's possible.

seven
Can I Carry Any Part of My College Experience into the Real World?

So far in this book, twentysomethings have described the difficulties they have had with shaping their adult identities. They have talked about pain and euphoria, confusion and revelation, apathy and determination. But what they have not yet discussed specifically is the root of the quarterlife crisis—the reason that all of these conflicting emotions and complex directions generally come into play when people are in their third decade. As we explained in the introduction, the catalyst for these problems is graduation from a school into whatever people call what happens afterward.

One of the reasons the trouble with this transition comes so unexpectedly is that during adolescence it is generally drilled into people that there is a natural progression from childhood to adulthood—that between high school and the real world there is this nexus called college that serves as the ideal in-between stage. Because the four (or more) years offer time away from home and a significant measure of self-reliance, it is assumed that, just as high school prepares students for college, so, too does college help prepare students for adulthood.

But, as scores of twentysomethings told us, that's not always the case. Academic material, newfound study habits, and the ability to heat soup do not necessarily translate into the next stage of life.

Actually, the way that many twentysomethings describe the shift out of college mode sounds less like a progressive stage than like the abrupt awakening experienced by that Rip Van Winkle of our time, Austin Powers (evacuation complete). Without much prior warning, it suddenly hits twentysomethings that they must adjust to an entirely new protocol to which they have hardly been exposed. The extent of the recovery period, of course, depends on the individual, sometimes the college, and how similar the school's environment is to the graduate's next port of call. And graduates' attitudes—toward both school and life afterward—can vary dramatically. But no matter how much they had been looking forward to life beyond a campus setting, nearly all of the twentysomethings in this book could think of something difficult and unexpected that they encountered after graduation for which college had not prepared them.

Six Degrees of Separation

Perhaps the most widespread assumption about college is that it best prepares students because it is a segue to the working world. That may be true for people who go into certain careers, such as medicine, because premed undergraduate courses might set up future doctors for medical school training, which in turn teaches students in stages as their white coats get incrementally longer. Moreover, on paper at least, it certainly doesn't hurt job applicants to be able to put some sort of bachelor's degree on their résumés. But, as several former students have found out, the work they had to perform in order to obtain their degrees often can be entirely different from the work that is necessary to get the jobs they desire. So when a prospective employer tells a recent graduate that he is not qualified for the job because he has no experience, the graduate often wonders why on earth he just spent four years working for a degree. Twentysomethings' frustration with this "catch 22"—that you need experience to gain experience, but employers will not offer the chance to gain experience unless you already have experience—can be an agonizing part of the quarterlife crisis. A resulting common view, as more than one twentysomething articulated, is "I didn't go to college to be a secretary."

"I went to an all-women's college where they taught you that you can do anything you want," says Maria, a 26-year-old in Seattle. "And that's how my whole life was up until college. Anything I wanted, I worked hard to achieve and did well at. Suddenly, I was getting rejection letters. And I thought, 'Wait a minute, I worked hard for that, I wanted that, and you said no?' I got into my college of choice, and every time I ran for any office at college, I got it. Now in the real world people are saying no to me, and that's a new experience. In college you reap the benefits— you work hard, you get an A, and everybody's happy. Here you work hard and they can still say, 'You just don't work for us.' I'm in a city where master's degrees are a dime a dozen; it doesn't make me an exception from anyone else. And that alone can put a big doubt in your head when you go for interviews and people tell you that you're not what they're looking for—but they have a secretary position."

Josh, a 1999 graduate of Willamette University (Salem, Oregon), says he had expected his job search to be much easier because unemployment is supposedly so low. But instead, he is having a tough time because he doesn't have the requisite level of experience. "I'm doing my own personal job search, which has been difficult," he says. "A lot of jobs are very set as to how many years of experience they need. If you don't have the three years of experience along with your college degree, you have to go with entry-level stuff. If you had gone with that job out of high school you could have gotten a better job by now. I wish they'd look at my college degree more seriously."

When 27-year-old Stacy graduated from college, she quickly realized that a degree in English was not nearly enough to qualify her for entry-level positions in the fields she wanted to pursue: journalism and writing. Not even four years of experience on her college newspaper counted as the "experience" required in the employment pages. Instead of interviewing sources, she is answering telephones; instead of writing articles, she is typing memos. "Outside of working for some tiny, small-town newspaper (hardly an option in my city), I am having trouble finding a job that I want without the requisite 'three to five years' experience preferred,'" she says. "I know that I could do many jobs well for which I am not necessarily qualified on paper. But because my résumé isn't as meaty as the human resources department would like, I haven't gotten as much as a phone call. The jobs for which I'm qualified usually involve various administrative tasks, much like the one I'm in right now. I'm beginning to feel that I need either a lot of luck or to find an organization or company that I want to work for, take any job, and hopefully get promoted within."

Part of Stacy's trouble is that she is mired in the experience "catch 22." But another part of it is that because she has no experience, the only jobs she can get right now are administrative positions that offer very little opportunity to acquire new skills. Without acquiring new skills, the only experience Stacy is gaining right now is in secretarial work, which she has no intention of pursuing. Stuck in the entry-level swamp, Stacy is like many driven, ambitious, well-educated recent graduates who get increasingly annoyed because of their drab job prospects. "I answer the phones for a United States Senator. I have various other rote tasks, but basically I am a bona fide receptionist," she says. "You would think that a job on Capitol Hill is relatively prestigious and that there are a lot of opportunities for promotion here, especially given the fast turnover rate on the Hill and the general transience in Washington. But although it sounds glamorous, it's really not. Meanwhile, my current job isn't giving my résumé the experience that an employer outside of the Hill would want to see. So I feel as though I am wasting my time, which is incredibly frustrating."

Likewise, when Kristina graduated in 1995 from Rollins College (Winter Park, Florida), as a double major in international business and management, she was unable to find a company willing to let her utilize the practical knowledge she had learned on her way to her seemingly marketable degrees. All of the positions offered to her revolved around typing, answering telephones, faxing, and filing. Essentially, she would have been an overqualified receptionist. "When I graduated from college, I thought getting a job would be a snap, because that's the impression we got from the career counselors and everyone around us. Boy, was I wrong," Kristina says. "For the first six months after school, I couldn't even get an administrative position. Granted, I was living in a little town in Louisiana at the time, so there weren't that many places to work. Gradually, I started feeling very lousy, so before I got totally depressed, I decided to get out of Louisiana and moved to a larger city. But it was the same story: no one wanted to hire me."

Kristina temped for a while, doing basic administrative work that eventually led to an account representative position at a company that shut down three months after she joined. In the string of similar jobs that followed, she was downsized because of her relative lack of experience. Finally she gave up and accepted a secretarial position. While she felt it was demeaning to work as a secretary despite her four years of college and her impressive-sounding degree, what became a brief stint as a secretary led to an administrative position that exposed her to the World Wide Web. Soon afterward, she became a Webmaster. "After three years of layoffs, depression, unemployment checks, and low-level administrative positions, here I am in computers," she says. "This is the last thing I thought I would be doing, but I love it. It was luck that got me where I am. I learned the hard way that getting the college diploma is not everything. I still am not sure if this is what I want to do, and I don't know if I ever will be sure, but for now this keeps the bills paid."

Kristina says she was fortunate because, although she was in an administrative position, someone recognized her potential and offered her the chance to learn new things and take on new responsibilities, which paved her way to a career in Web development. It took her three years, however, to realize that a job below her standards probably was not worth taking unless it offered her the opportunity to acquire skills that would benefit her future search for the job she really wanted. Kristina says she tried to follow the advice of her college career counselor, who merely said that everything would eventually fall into place. It would have made sense if the career counselor had instead explained basic strategies instead of giving airy platitudes to students, but, as many twentysomethings told us, most college career services centers—even, and perhaps especially, at some of the top-tier universities in the country—hardly offer anything of use. It is interesting that these "service" centers simply do not prepare students who will have to put in some service time of their own before they will be able to climb into the career of their choice. Not surprisingly, college career centers are generally more than happy to assist students who want to apply for fellowships, grants, postgraduate scholarships, or prestigious awards—award-winning students translate into successful college career services centers, which reflects well on the schools. Generally, the career centers facilitate the on-campus recruiting system and subsequently aid the students who want to go into consulting, investment banking, and, in some cases, technology careers. But they leave the rest of the student body—future artists, teachers, actors, carpenters, writers, musicians, politicians, engineers, and everybody else—by the wayside.

Essentially, the career centers help students prepare their résumés, but they don't suggest what to do with them. The standard rosy pamphlets they make available often include sample cover letters and perhaps some resources for further research, but nothing more than what students can find in the hundreds of books on the market that offer step-by-step instructions on how to apply for a job. If career centers would just tell it like it is—that recent graduates might have to "put in their time" by doing administrative work, that they could be in for some emotional turmoil when they have to lower their standards, that their ideal jobs may have nothing to do with their majors—then twenty-somethings might be better prepared.

Another factor that leads to some twentysomethings' job-related stress is that, because they didn't major in a subject directly relevant to their jobs, they feel like fakes. Courtney, 25, says she felt like she was just going through the motions when she got her first job out of college. "I always doubted myself and my abilities because I didn't know how I got the job. I still think it was a fluke," she says. "I never even gave them my transcript. The way I got the first interview was just snaky on my part. They were having an informational session at school and I wanted a free hat, so I left without staying for the informational session. Then when I left I wondered, 'What is this whole consulting thing about?' Afterward, I got a phone call from them, so from the beginning it was like it was fake. I was the only person who had no computer experience. I was the only political science major ever to be hired there as best I could tell. So I completely felt like I didn't fit in intellectually into their business mold. That took years to deal with. I was the biggest fluke ever. I don't even know what my GPA is—I almost flunked out my freshman year. I really wasn't qualified."

Batting for the Majors

Elaine, a 24-year-old from Dallas, says that for her, one of the most frustrating aspects of college career centers, the postcollege recruiting process, and the general hiring system was to see the "over-the-top emphasis" on business majors. "At the start, I believed this group was self-selective—that those who really wanted to work in business were those who had spent their undergraduate years majoring in business or economics," she says. "Later, I found that this was only partly true. From my experience as a job applicant and then as part of a hiring team, I was always horrified when individuals were passed over simply because they had not majored in what I consider to be the least challenging and most mindless majors of any college. This specificity ideal is apparent not only when reviewing majors but also when reviewing work experience. Who knows, as a twentysomething or as a college intern, what specific kind of marketing, or which financial desk, or which business technologies will appeal most? Why should an intern position be judged simply on its corporate reputation? Why do people want 24-year-olds to be experts at anything? Specialization is a disease. It paralyzes young professionals, preventing them from taking risks at jobs that will not blend in with their résumés. And college never prepared us for—and in fact fought against—this real-world ideal. Besides," Elaine adds, "even when a course or a major seems superficially to prepare you for a particular job role, it only does so superficially."

When recent graduates have been lucky enough to find jobs in vaguely the same field as their college majors, they can still encounter unpleasant surprises when they discover the work they will actually be doing. At MIT (Cambridge, Massachusetts), 24-year-old Amanda says she muddled through her work because her only goal was to move on into the world beyond campus life. "In college, I never knew what I wanted to study and never got really into anything, so I feel like I just passed on through and graduated. I thought the real world was where it was at. I don't know if that's still true," she says. After she graduated with a degree in economics, she got what she considered to be a respectable researcher position at an economic consulting firm. The job appealed to her because she would be working with other recent graduates and because she believed it would give her a chance to apply her degree to her work. On paper, the job description made it appear to be something for which she was intellectually qualified because the work seemed substantial. In reality, the job disappoints Amanda because it consists of menial tasks that she feels do not require much thought, let alone the kind of thought refined by a degree in economics. "Essentially, a monkey could do my job—they must hire us smart students for the five percent of the time that we are actually using our brains," she says.

Marnel, who got a job similar to Amanda's after graduating from Hanover College (Indiana) with a degree in economics in 1994, also has been disappointed with how he has not truly been able to apply his field of study. In his current position as an economic researcher, Marnel spends most of his time on the computer. He says that the work he does, speculating consumer trends, is just not vital enough to the world to fulfill him. "Right now I'm pointing and clicking all day," Marnel says. "I was interested in economics and enjoyed the courses in college, but I found out after graduation that studying economics is a lot different than actually working in the field. I guess I didn't realize what it meant to be doing economic research, which was what I could do after college. I was a little naive going into the field because at school I'd never done research full time. I like working with computers, economics, and quantitative fields, but now I know I don't want to do it for a long-term career. The job has made me more cynical because I think a lot of economics is detached from reality. A lot of things they try to measure, like human behavior, are impossible to predict. And in economics you have to make a lot of assumptions. I often wonder why we're doing this stuff."

Marnel says that even though his job is not too demanding and requires only forty hours a week, which is far fewer hours than many of his friends have to work, he still had a tough time adjusting to the working world in general. "I didn't enter too intense a work environment, but it's difficult to move from going to school full time—where I just sat in lectures for a couple of hours a day, absorbing information without having to be on or producing something—to a job where I'm working eight hours a day." Marnel has been so discouraged by the jobs available in the field he studied in college that he has applied for medical school (where he can revisit those lectures he misses so much). He has given up entirely on finding a satisfying job that is related to his degree.

Precisely because she felt that students created a tougher twenty-something transition for themselves when they rushed through college just to graduate without taking the energy to figure out which major would truly help them, Victoria, a 25-year-old who lives in New York City, decided to take her time in college. "Like most kids, I jumped into undergraduate studies with the hopes of finishing a college degree in four years. A degree in what? I had no idea. So I became the Intro Queen, enrolling in what seemed like every introductory course offered at Purdue University. Needless to say, my parents weren't pleased that I was choosing classes in the same fashion I would select food from a buffet," Victoria says. "I started asking people how they knew what they wanted to study. Their answers surprised me. Some chose majors merely at the suggestion of someone else, others at the demands of their parents. One thing became very apparent: very few selected a major because it was something they were genuinely interested in. I was certain this wouldn't be me. After doing some long, hard thinking, I realized that I wasn't going to choose a degree or career simply to graduate in four years. If I was going to continue with college, I would have to determine what I was passionate about. I didn't care how long it would take. In my sophomore year I chose to pursue a career in medicine."

When Victoria told her father her plans, he said that she didn't have what it took to become a doctor. "Know your limitations," he told her. "Whatever. Do most 19-year-olds know what their limitations are?" she says. "I went through a period of depression following that conversation with my father. All sorts of questions flooded my mind. What the hell was I going to do with my life? Why did everyone else around me seemingly know what they wanted to do with their lives? Why did it feel like I was two steps behind everyone else?" During this time of emotional upheaval, Victoria's grade point average plummeted until she arrived at the decision to go to nursing school instead. After three years of college, she transferred into another university's nursing program, even though it meant she would have to move to a new school in a major city and start all over again. College would be a seven-year plan. "While I felt positive about this decision, I still had my doubts. How did I know this would work out? What if it didn't? I was going on my instincts, but I still didn't trust myself," she says.

In her new city, Victoria immediately got a job in a hematology lab at a local hospital so that she could set up contacts who might be able to help her land a nursing job when she graduated. But the worst hit came when she failed her boards. "It was a major blow. I had rearranged my life to become a nurse," she says. "I did well in school. I knew this was what I was meant to be doing. Why didn't I pass? My father's words were echoing in my ears: 'Know your limitations.' Was I not smart enough for medicine? My God, I had just completely failed at what I had set out to do. I was ready to run—really run. Thoughts of going out to the West Coast to live in a hut on the beach and smoke tons of pot were very appealing. I was scared to death, completely depressed, and spiraling downward. Nothing anyone said to encourage me was effective."

After a few weeks of sulking, she decided to be more proactive than reactive. She enrolled in a board review course, graduated with a 4.0 average, and finally passed the boards. She thought she was all set to move on to the workforce. But, she says, "I was wrong when I thought things would only be on the up-and-up from there. My first nursing job left much to be desired. It was not the kind of nursing I wanted to be practicing. The administration and management were unsupportive and nurses were carrying patient loads that were unsafe. The stress was unbearable and I was miserable. So, since my previous life experiences had taught me that change is growth and that being proactive pays off, I went for yet another change. I got a new job at another hospital. It rocks and I am finally happy. At 25, those feelings of self-doubt and uncertainty have diminished a bit. Hey, it's been a long seven years. But knowing that it took a lot of hard work and perseverance to get to where I am today gives me a higher level of self-satisfaction. Does it matter that it took me almost seven years to obtain a bachelor's degree? Absolutely not. I believe that 18-year-olds should wait to begin a four-year degree if they are uncertain of a major or career choice. If possible, why not travel or do two years at a junior college beforehand? If I had it to do all over again, I would have done both."

It took Victoria a long time to figure out exactly how she would best be able to utilize her degree once she graduated. Obviously, not all twentysomethings have the patience and foresight to plot out the next ten years of their lives while they are still in school. And, as Elaine said, very often college majors just don't translate into specific fields in the workforce. But sometimes recent graduates discover that they fell into a particular course of study in college for a reason, even if they initially thought their only real goal was to slide through school for the diploma. Sandra, a 25-year-old from Alabama, majored in business at a liberal arts school, where her training was limited. After school she went into an entirely different field and began a long stint in computers. Three years later, however, she decided to switch to a field that would make better use of her business knowledge. "In my new field of interior design, I'll probably eventually own my own business, in which case hopefully some of my business training will come in useful," Sandra says. "I've interviewed two interior decorators to get an idea of the business, and both were highly impressed by the business degree and said it would be a real asset."

Whatever the college major, Rick, a 1997 graduate of the University of Wisconsin–Madison, says that the only way he knows for twentysomethings to get out of the experience "catch 22" is to network. "It ain't easy, but finding a good position where you can learn something is not impossible. I had no internships to get the hands-on experience that employers were looking for, and it was frustrating," he says. "I have a master's in economics and I was answering phones. It fucking blew. But it's a connection (not to be confused with a start), and you pass your résumé to everyone and their uncle—*and follow up*. It only takes one person to see your résumé or for you to meet. The more people you meet, the more your chances increase of getting 'experience'—it's basic math. The worst thing to do is to settle and stop looking. Then (yes, like me) you will be answering phones for a while."

Look at All the Lonely People

Certainly work is not the only area in which real life differs greatly from the college scene. But when jobs don't necessarily continue anything relevant to the past sixteen years of a recent graduate's life, it often comes as a surprise to twentysomethings. What they do not find quite so startling—many times they have been warned—is the vast, mind-boggling change in their social lives. Michael, a 1998 graduate of Franklin and Marshall (Lancaster, Pennsylvania), says he had a tough transition period in the year between college and law school, partly because he wasn't making the money necessary to create opportunities to meet people. "Socially, in a frat in college, it was a lot easier to meet people of the opposite sex because of mixers with sororities," he says. "There were plenty of opportunities and parties in law school as well. It's much harder to meet people in the real world."

It will come as no big shocker that a steady social life can become more difficult after a twentysomething leaves the insulated college pod, which, as they are told over and over again (this usually goes along with the "college is the best four years of your life" speech), is the only place they will be able to live where they will be with so many other people in the same age range. Graduates already know this. What is harder for them to figure out is how to meet people after school, how much time and energy to put into meeting those people, and what to do once they have already met them—keeping in mind, among other things, their financial, geographical, and time constraints. Bill, a 1994 graduate of Pennsylvania State University (University Park), says he has had trouble finding buddies even though he moved to his current city years ago. "It's still hard to meet new guy friends. When guys already have a group of friends, it's hard to break in and become part of the group rather than a tag-along," he says.

One basic problem for twentysomethings is that, because they are so used to meeting people at school, after graduation they naturally fall into the habit of trying to meet people at work. Unfortunately, their standards are often so high because of the intense quality of the four-year relationships they formed in college that their relationships with colleagues do not quite match up. Kevin, who graduated in 1999 from Colgate University (Hamilton, New York), says that even though he moved to a place where he already felt comfortable, he didn't find it any easier to meet new people. "I knew I wouldn't stay with this job for that long, so I stayed in a familiar area. I know where to go to do things I enjoy here," he says. "But at work I've seen a lot of people who moved here for a job and now sit around wondering, 'What the hell do I do?' And the lab where I work does jack squat to help people meet and socialize. I'm 24 and single and out of college, and these are not the people I'm going to hang out with. I'm not going to make social connections on the job because there's nothing to encourage this. To me, that's tremendously frustrating. Luckily I'm in a better situation than some of the people I work with who are just out of college and don't know anybody or what's around here. Nothing is done to ease this transition."

But even when a company does offer an environment that encourages coworkers to socialize, recent graduates can be left wondering if this happy-hour mode of socialization is all there is left. Twenty-five-year-old Renée, who grew up, went to college, and now works in the Midwest, says that although her firm provides an atmosphere conducive to meeting people her age, she doesn't necessarily want all of her friends to share her office building. Plus, she says, she doesn't have much in common with her coworkers besides her age, her Midwestern background, and the fact that she works at that particular company. "One thing I miss from school is having intelligent friends to talk to all the time. All of my current friends I met through work or at work or they still work with me, and sometimes it's overkill," she says. "Sometimes I go out with people I spend fifty hours a week with, which is fine, and we manage for an hour or two not to talk about work, but it's easy to get lulled back into it. It's hard to meet anyone outside work. It's hard to find people with the same interests. If you don't work at a place with other young people, I can't imagine how to meet people. For instance, I joined a tennis league, which helps with meeting people, but beyond playing tennis I'm not good at carrying it on and taking that leap to doing stuff outside of tennis. Plus, I don't even know their last names. People just don't seem as interesting or diverse as the people I went to school with—they all seem the same. I miss that part of college. Everyone is at school for basically the same reasons and has been screened, and generally you know things about them. After school, meeting people is a trade-off: Do you keep pursuing people despite the fact that it's a lot of work, or is it better to end it? Because you don't know anything about them."

Meanwhile, like most twentysomethings in the twenty-first century, Renée maintains her college friendships through E-mail (hey, free long-distance). But technology doesn't help Renée with her quest to find a boyfriend—she can't E-mail him if she doesn't know him (though people like Jake, a 28-year-old from Kentucky, persistently defend the merits of cybersex). Like people in any age group, twentysomethings have a more difficult time meeting possible romantic partners than finding friends. But this trouble is much more pronounced for people who have just emerged from a school setting, where frequent instances of "hooking up" do not always signify promiscuity, and going home with someone on the first date seems, somehow, safer than it does as an adult—partly because, given the sheltered school setting, it is likely that a friend or a friend of a friend can vouch for that someone. As Amanda points out, "It's hard—everything is different and sketchy when it comes to meeting people. How do you know whom you can trust? In college, you knew someone in the other dorm was an economics major or whatever, and now it's harder to meet people through people. I've met people at clubs before and I kind of like it because then I know they're fun, but also I worry sometimes."

For Renée, the change between the structured socializing in college and the free-for-all afterward is reflected by adults' attitudes toward finding mates. "I think that's the worst part of not having the structure of college—not having a casual way to meet people. I've gone to some big mixer parties and there's a weird feeling in the air—lots of women on the hunt. You have to wonder about the quality of people who are out to hunt," she says. "It's really hard to meet guys, especially working in communications, because the majority of my coworkers are women. I don't feel like I need a guy to go anywhere. But although I feel self-actualized and interesting enough as a person, and my life is full, a boyfriend would be frosting on top of the cake. And sometimes I get bored. Not so bored that I can't find something to do, but it would be nice to call someone about my day, and even if it's mundane he's interested because it's me."

Nicole, a 25-year-old in Buffalo, says that now that she has seen how difficult it is to meet possible romantic partners after graduation, she realizes she should have put forth more of an effort while she was in college. "I can't decide when I should get married and have kids— and I change my mind every day—but I'm definitely looking for a relationship. Meanwhile, I can't meet people at work, and it's hard to meet people outside of work. I wish I tried harder to meet people in college, because it was easier to meet people and we had a lot more in common. I think people should spend more time doing that in college than studying," she says.

Twentysomethings don't really have any practical, universal solutions for the "how to meet someone" question. On the contrary, most of them say they just happened to meet their significant others when they weren't really looking. "It's a lot harder to meet people in the real world because there isn't such a plethora of scheduled events," says Joel, a 1993 graduate of Dartmouth College (Hanover, New Hampshire). "And now you're working all day and you come home tired and try to find the energy to meet people. I met my fiancée by chance, on the metro, as we were both headed home. It turned out we lived in the same apartment building. I had previously tried a lot of those singles group things. I went to the Jewish community's single adults center, and it was me and a bunch of old men. They were all single, but really not the type I was looking for."

Patrick, a 1998 University of Michigan (Ann Arbor) graduate, says he found an easy, if odd, way to meet people: he left the country. "In college, because I was an immature git, I spent most of my free time playing beer pong in my fraternity house, which didn't get me out to meet new folks much," he says. "Now, though, I'm on a program for native English speakers in rural Japan. I live in the Japanese version of Appalachia, so there are virtually no foreigners except about seventy-five in the program, whose rules restrict participants to being between ages 22 and 35. Every year, some leave and new ones come up, and as former head of the professional association in this prefecture, I meet most of them right off the plane. (I'm going down to Tokyo next week to bring up a new batch.) Furthermore, I stand out like a sore thumb. I am one of three non-Asians in my town of twenty thousand. Meeting new people who want to know what I think of the town, or of Japan generally, or whether I would like to come over for dinner, is something I have to fend off rather than search for. I expect, though, that when I go back to the States next year, things will get tougher. All my college friends report it so. Maybe I'll stay in Japan."

Lifestyle Changes

Perhaps the biggest problem for recent graduates is that they have to adjust to an entirely different lifestyle—one that involves work, social life, new financial circumstances, and other aspects of the postcollege world. After several years of being catered to by family members and school officials, suddenly twentysomethings have to figure things out for themselves in a world that mostly still believes that the twenties are the easiest years of adulthood. There are no safety nets after graduation.

"The transition just didn't seem real," says Ashley, a 1997 graduate of Brown University (Providence, Rhode Island). "I kept waiting for spring break, or winter break, or summer. After a while it never happened. And I think I still sort of expect it to happen, but it never does. I don't think it sunk in for a long time that I actually had to go to work and this is my life. I went out all the time when I first graduated from college. Even up to a year after I graduated I'd go out every night. Now, so many nights I prefer to sit home and watch a movie." Part of the prescription, of course, is time—it takes experience as an adult to know how to act like one. But meanwhile, that does not make the transition any easier. "I believe twentysomethings experience a difficult time transitioning from college to the real world because they are not prepared," says Claudia, a 1997 graduate of St. Lawrence University (Canton, New York). "As much as my undergraduate education taught me, there are certain life experiences it did not prepare me for at all. I think people enjoy the support systems in place at college, but then are left to fend for themselves after graduation. College does not teach you these lessons. Real life does."

Rick, the 1997 University of Wisconsin graduate, says this lack of preparation can be directly attributed to a failure on the part of institutions of higher learning to school the students on topics that really matter. He blames universities for twentysomethings' troubles because, rather than nudge graduates into adulthood, they coddle them so that they regress into childhood. "College should be the gateway to independence, but the trend in America contradicts that with cushier schools at higher prices," he says. "I even read an article about a school where room service was an option. Whatever happened to dingy rooms, food shopping, cooking, cleaning—you know, all that real-world, independent stuff that you're supposed to pick up in college? And professors practically beg students to get papers in on time and give extensions and give warnings about 'tough' questions. I studied a year and a half in Germany and Spain. I found that experience much more helpful now that I'm out on my own. You had to find a place on your own, go to class on your own (professors care less if you show up or not—it's your life anyway, right?); there were more bars instead of sheltered campus parties where no locals are allowed to mingle. But that's why we pay all that money for college—protection from the real world. It's not a slow embrace of the real world, even though that should be the goal."

A frustrating adjustment in lifestyle for many twentysomethings is the change in structure after college or graduate school. While there may have been a set agenda in place in school that directed students toward the end goal of graduating with a degree, daily schedules were never so rigid that they were set in stone. The real world reverses that dichotomy because there is no underlying directive, no umbrella under which recent graduates are supposed to operate, but at the same time they are expected to work under someone else's schedule. "Most people I know in a similar situation feel the same way: that transitioning from college to the real world has been tremendously difficult because basically you have to leave an environment where you're free to do what you want all day long," says Kevin, the 1999 Colgate University graduate. "You have classes and responsibilities, but they're flexible. If you're feeling tired, you can skip a class and catch up. You can grab food when you want it, you can go to sleep at whatever time you want to, depending on what you want to do that day. Then you transition from that to a world where you have to wake up and be at work at a certain time. Me, I have to sit on my ass for eight hours a day, sometimes without any work, but I have to be there anyway. No one can work for eight hours straight. I sit there and wonder, why am I sitting here wasting my time? I wish I could be doing something else. In college I had the flexibility to do that. If I couldn't concentrate, I'd go to the gym, go running, or hang out for a while, and then get back to the problem. But at work you sit there, and you might do E-mail or make phone calls, but it's not an environment conducive to free thinking. On the psychological front, it's frustrating, very discouraging, and not rewarding. It seems really pointless, and it's strange that I paid $10,000 dollars a year for five years to be trained in exactly the wrong way. It would have made a lot more sense to go from high school to a job than to college, because the environment is so different. For most people, in high school you would basically sit down for six or seven hours every day, and you would study, do your work, break for lunch, and everything was very much scheduled and set. Then, for four or five years in college, you're trained to completely abandon all that training and try to do as well as you can in an environment that encourages a very flexible mentality. It's difficult to plan anything in college. And then, oh, you go right back to the very regimental workday. It just doesn't seem like all the money I spent on college was worth it."

For Kevin personally, the shift from a college environment to a job environment was tough because he simply didn't realize what was coming. "In college, you're not really encouraged to explore what jobs are out there. And even when you do get an internship, if you're fortunate enough, most of the time it's not a realistic reflection of that job. I had an internship at IBM where I did very little stuff, so I didn't get a good feeling for it. It was a waste of three months, although I got some money," he says. Now, in his current job, he is having a difficult time dealing with the fact that he does not have clear-cut projects, with clear beginnings, clear ends, and clear results, like he did in college. Then again, there is also the problem that he is not one of those people who can sit still and get things done in large blocks of time. "It's very hard—the guilt, the tremendous guilt—like the fact that I can't sit there at work for eight hours and be productive the entire day. I feel horrible when I go home because I feel like I haven't accomplished anything. The worst part is now that it's been about a year and those feelings of guilt have diminished, I feel like my productivity has pretty much slowed to a crawl. I'm therefore very unsatisfied with my job. I feel like I should be going back to school this fall."

Kevin doesn't have a quick solution to combat the hard-hitting nature of this lifestyle shift, but he does hope that, in this constantly changing working world, companies will soon realize how important it is to accommodate new hires just out of school and take some of the responsibility for the symptoms of the quarterlife crisis. As opposed to previous decades, when jobs were relatively hard to come by (so if twentysomethings had a decent position, they dealt with whatever employers threw at them), the presently low unemployment rates, Kevin says, should drive employers to bend over backwards to make sure their rookies are comfortable. He says that all of his company's new hires with whom he spoke told him they were finding it extremely difficult to sit still for eight hours straight and were therefore experiencing a major reduction in productivity. "Currently, people are hopping jobs every year, mostly because they're not satisfied with the job that they have. To me, from a financial standpoint, it would make a lot of sense if a company realized that this transition is really hard, and put forth a lot of effort to make the transition easier and to actually help their employees, as opposed to just sticking more meat in the grinder," he says. "I get the feeling that that would breathe loyalty and be beneficial in the long run. But no one seems to have a clue about this and once you get eight years out of college, you don't remember what this was like. It's just forgotten. It would be an amazing edge if a company came up to me and said they had a program in place to help my transition from college, with a flexible work environment. So if I don't want to work forty hours a week but instead have to do a certain amount of work every week—and even if I need to work from home—that's fine, because they are flexible as long as I get the work done. With that kind of treatment early on, to encourage and help me develop and grow as an employee right out of school, I'd start to think about being loyal to that company. It's just disappointing that no one's got a clue. They need to find a way to make this transition smoother."

Meanwhile, people like Will, a 1995 graduate of the University of Richmond (Virginia), are trying to learn on their own how to move from college party mode to serious worker mode, which is a more confusing move than it sounds like it should be. The trouble, besides the awareness that it is just something they should do, is that there isn't much motivation for twentysomethings to make that change in the first place—unless, as in Will's case, they will be fired if they don't. In Will's first job out of college, he did technical support for a company from one P.M. to eleven P.M. and then drank with friends throughout the night. He says it was like being paid to go to college. When the work became tiresome, he got a new job that gave him more responsibility and taught him new skills, such as public speaking. But Will didn't realize that with the new hours and the new responsibilities, he had to change his slacker attitude. "Socially, I could apply thirty to forty percent of what I learned in college to what I was doing in my first job. In my second job it was more like ten percent," he says. "What became difficult for me was balancing between 'Hey, let's go out and booze all night' and 'I got to be at work at nine.' So I struggled with that. It took me a while to balance it."

One night Will was out having a couple of beers with a supervisor who noticed that Will's nocturnal partying habits were (surprise) having a direct effect on his productivity at work in the morning. As Will puts it, he got in trouble for living the college life when he wasn't in college anymore. "I was not totally ready for the maturity aspect of what was presented to me at this job. I was basically not ready to be an adult," he says. "So I was given the choice to either continue to be a slacker and be fired or shape up and don't get fired. Being the smart idiot I was, I didn't get fired. At this point, I've been out of college for five years and I'm still like, 'Hey, let's go party,' but at the same time I realize I have to be at work tomorrow morning. It's a difficult thing to balance the social aspect as well as the work aspect. I was a slacker in college and now I'm supposed to be a respected adult."

Just because Will has gotten used to the idea of not being a slacker, though, doesn't mean that he has adjusted to the idea of working for a large company rather than for himself. Many twentysomethings are disappointed to find that a job offers a lot less glamour than they had expected, but they can be downright devastated when they realize that sometimes, in the large scheme of things in the working world, who they are and what they do does not necessarily matter. "After four years at this job, I'm actually pretty pissed off at where I am now," Will says. "The company I started working for was fun, small, hip, happening. Now it's a regular corporate environment. I'm a cog in the wheel. I'm a person who sits there and instead of being person XYZ I became employee number 21335. I'm no longer somebody who's recognized as being a person."

Claudia also encountered problems when she tried to treat the years after graduation as a direct continuation of her undergraduate years. "I found a job in a major city near my university and thought I'd be absolutely happy. I was in a great city with tons of young professionals, a hot night life, and friends living minutes away. However, I imagined my life as an extension of college, and it was far from it. Learning to adjust to a work lifestyle with late nights and no afternoon naps took some time to get used to. I learned that plans with friends could not

Can I Carry Any Part of My College
Experience into the Real World?

be made spontaneously; instead, they had to be planned a week in advance." Miserable, Claudia decided that the only way to accept the fact that she was not in college anymore was to move as far away from it as possible and start again.

Continuing Education

There is no magic solution, but some twentysomethings told us that they have actually discovered an ideal way both to prolong their college lifestyle and to smooth the transition afterward. It doesn't make for a seamless move from college into the real world, but graduate school has enough elements of both worlds, twentysomethings say, that it has the potential to work pretty well. Several recent college graduates use graduate school as something of a stall tactic because they are nostalgic for the undergraduate days, because they don't feel they are ready for adulthood, or because they just don't know what they want to do with the rest of their lives. The downside to all of this is that graduate school costs money, and for a twentysomething to spend that money (or his parents' money) just for the sake of going to graduate school may not actually ease the inevitable transition into adulthood—if the twentysomething does not know what he wants to do before graduate school, years of study in a field he doesn't feel strongly about might not change that problem.

Justine, a 1997 graduate of the University of Utah (Salt Lake City), went to graduate school essentially to extend her college career, but found out once she got there that graduate school was instead more of an in-between stage following college and preceding the real world. "In some ways graduate school is like going back to college, because it's nice to be around students again, but in other ways I felt like a freshman," she says. "At college I'd always see people I knew, but when I saw someone I knew at grad school it was a big deal. I felt like in grad school I was on the other side of it, working with professors in the office. In college, my professors were only people I'd get grades from—I didn't establish relationships with them. In grad school I did, and it was interesting being in school and realizing I was more grown up as opposed to having fun and trying to get by, because I was taking things more seriously now."

To try to make her graduate school experience more like college, Justine became the social chair for the school's student government. She organized things like happy hours, but it was difficult to spread the word because, she says, the graduate students were basically engrossed in their own departments. "In some ways, it definitely isn't the same as college," she says. "First of all, the social life is different because you're more involved in your studies than you were back in college, when there was more time for having a social life. There is a different mentality than as an undergraduate in terms of the dynamics of school and what's expected of you. We've already been through the whole college experience, so it's harder to repeat it because we're more tired and we have more commitments, like full-time jobs, whereas in college most people's only job is to be in school. I didn't have many friends who worked in college. And also, you're in smaller classes that are more engaging and thought-provoking. You're not just sitting through lectures and jotting down responses; you're going home, reading about a topic, and then discussing it with the class. And you're figuring out the material, trying to apply it to your life, placing it in different scenarios, asking questions, and getting the full attention of both the professor and your peers. Grad school is definitely more relevant to the real world. It gave me new interests, and now I have fewer hang-ups and fewer things to go through and figure out."

For Mike, a 1995 graduate of Emory University (Atlanta), graduate school served as an introduction to some of the challenges he would have to learn to face as an adult. And it worked—he said his transition from Tufts to Emory Law School was a difficult one, which made his move from law school to the real world all that much easier. "Law school was a tough reality," he says. "Going from second semester senior year of college, which is a fun time in people's lives, to the first year of law school, which is harsh, was a tough transition to make. I had to work at making school a priority more than ever before, and also at making friends. In law school, people were at different stages in their lives, at different ages, with different perspectives and agendas. Some people were more self-serving than others, so it took a while to make friends with people who were supportive of their classmates as opposed to other people who were competitive and trying to one-up themselves the whole time. So I ended up making some great friends, but it took time to weed out the good people from the bad. In college, we were all excited to be there when we were freshmen, but in law school, not so much. Law school was a good transition in terms of being in a new environment with new challenges, introducing me to new kinds of people, and opening my eyes to new kinds of experiences."

For Joel, the transition from college to law school was also tough, but he was able to view the shift with a more mature perspective than most twentysomethings because of his extenuating circumstances: he had a brain tumor. "It was different for me because in my junior year I developed a very rare brain tumor that affected my vision and hearing. I went on to law school after graduating, but my big concerns then were adjusting to having different vision and a different sense of hearing, which were not typical concerns that a lot of people have after school. For me the transition was more about dealing with the tumor than about the notion of college being over. It was hard but liberating, because by then I was finally feeling like I was healthy enough to go to law school," he says.

It might have been this different perspective that encouraged Joel to adjust to the transition gradually and on his own time. Furthermore, he was also better equipped to deal with law school than other students might have been because he moved closer to his family. "The big difference between college and law school was that I had my family close by at school because my father's a professor there. But I was also in a new city with a really hard law school. I went from a very small town to a large city, so I was still dealing with living in the city where people cut you off and they're not all that friendly. I was a little overwhelmed by crowds on subways," he says. "It was a gradual transition because I started out in the law school dorm my first year, and had to do some cooking on my own, and then moved to apartments, so everything came gradually—nothing too traumatic. Having to cook my own food was hard, as opposed to being able to sign up for a meal plan. That was hard—forget about the cancer—just the notion that there was no life meal plan. There are still days when I think about, instead of cooking dinner, how nice it would be if I could just go back to college. The dining was just exceptional. People like it and look forward to it and really miss it when they move away. That's one of the harder things—that and cleaning your own bathroom."

As a result of his graduate school experience, Joel felt that he was more ready for the real world than he might have been had he not gone to law school. "I got to a point where I was very tired of being lectured to, in undergrad and law school, and in the hospital," he says. "I was ready to stop being taught. And for a while it was nice to be working. But then I missed the ability to schedule classes from nine to one on Tuesdays and Thursdays, and to have six-day weekends."

What You Can Take with You

Fortunately, twentysomethings do admit that, despite their frustrations with it, the college experience is not all for nothing. There are some aspects of undergraduate life that recent graduates believe can help them when they graduate. For example, Cathy, a 23-year-old in White Plains, New York, says that college did actually teach her to be more of an adult than a child. "I think the thing to carry from college is how to meet and relate well to other people," she says. "Yeah, academics help somewhat, but college is where we learn to be mature social beings, which is necessary for life in the real world."

Perhaps the most specifically relevant aspect of college that twenty-somethings can directly apply to life in the real world is best articulated by Lauren, a 26-year-old graduate of Northwestern University (Evanston, Illinois). Lauren says that her incredible ability to procrastinate, a vital skill that she spent hours refining in college, has been crucial to easing her adjustment into the working world. "After my first three years in the workforce, I can honestly say that I learned some very practical skills in college that have helped me survive in a fast-paced environment," she says. "In college, I was the biggest procrastinator. I know that this is not necessarily a good thing, but by learning to study and write at the last minute, I have been able to meet every deadline ever given to me, even on short notice. Of course, I retained some knowledge of the subjects I studied in school, and my public speaking class was helpful, but the actual experience of working under pressure has proven to be the most beneficial in my current position." Lauren's observation is fitting, because the one thing that many twentysomethings do when they realize how little they can actually take with them from college to the rest of their lives, is stall. College, clearly, doesn't quite cut it anymore.

conclusion

When we told 90-year-old Irving that we were writing this book about the quarterlife crisis, he agreed that the idea of a twentysomething counterpart to the midlife crisis seems accurate. But then he added that he believes people experience some sort of crisis in every decade. So we asked him, partly in jest, what the ninetysomething crisis involves. He paused for only a few seconds before he responded, "Finding interesting activities to do. And learning to deal with the fact that many of your friends are gone."

Our breaths caught in our throats.

Here we were, writing about a crisis to which some critics would merely respond, "Stop whining and just deal with it," while people who just dealt with it three quarters of a century ago are confronting and surviving a much more striking and permanent pain. Twentysomethings might be anxious about finding the people who are going to be their lifelong friends. But ninetysomethings are anxious about losing them. The latter must be infinitely more difficult.

We realized, however, that our point is not that the twentysomething years comprise the most difficult crisis that adults experience.
We are only suggesting that the quarterlife crisis is at least as important,
widespread, and strenuous as the midlife crisis, and therefore deserves
the same kind of recognition. The years that one of our twentysomething sources described as the limbo between "young adult" and "adult"
are hard, but they are hard in part because the rest of the population
believes they are so easy. There are many advantages to being a twentysomething, surely, but people know about those. What they do not
acknowledge is that there is a dark side as well. Because no one ever
talks about this dark side, twentysomethings are surprised when they
encounter it, and discouraged when they believe they are the only ones
who experience it. This is a circuitous cycle of secrecy, like those six
friends of Ryan's who approached him under the strictest confidentiality, one by one, to seek his advice about their depression; because they
were afraid of what their other best friends would say, they never knew
that their entire circle was experiencing the same crisis.

In the Introduction, we mentioned how various cultures have always
used different means to mark and to ease the transition from childhood
to adulthood. At some point during the past two centuries, North Americans came to view the college experience as a sufficient stand-in for
this rite of passage. Has it worked in the past? Probably. Has it continued to work? No. As scores of people who have graduated within
the past ten years told us over and over again, times have changed,
twentysomethings have changed, and the transition has changed. The
quarterlife crisis is only getting worse as we progress into the twenty-
first century, and the only way to begin to alleviate it is to acknowledge
that it exists.

Many twentysomethings mentioned that they would like to join some sort of support group for recent graduates. If you would like access to information about support groups, resources, and discussion forums for twentysomethings, please visit www.quarterlifecrisis.com

Appendix

So you've read the book. Now what?

Some of you may have pulled through your quarterlife crisis simply by realizing that you are not alone. Pondering these types of issues is a normal and often inevitable part of being in your twenties; and knowing that other twentysomethings go through the same experience can decrease your self-doubt. For others of you, however, reading this book might be only the first step in a longer process of making peace with yourselves. Perhaps we can at least give you a head start.

Without a doubt, the most important thing you can do to cope with and move beyond your quarterlife crisis is to talk about it. A few years ago, if you had tried to bring up serious identity issues with twenty-somethings, you might have gotten some strange looks. Now, however, you have a widely accepted, easily recognizable, and droll party line that serves to spark important discussions about issues that no one used to talk about. "Hey, I think I'm having a quarterlife crisis," you say to your friends. "What do I do?" You might be surprised at the sympathy, stories, and suggestions you hear in response.

Of course, starting that kind of conversation in a random place isn't always easy. Opening that discussion in a group designed to combat the quarterlife crisis, however, is. Fortunately, many of your peers have expressed interest in joining and/or forming quarterlife crisis support groups.

www.quarterlifecrisis.com, the official *Quarterlife Crisis* website, acts as the headquarters to a network of support groups forming around the world. *Quarterlife Crisis* support groups offer the opportunities to befriend others in similar situations and to discuss personal and professional problems in an open and supportive environment. These forums continue the aim of this book, which is to reassure you that your anxieties are increasingly common.

Quarterlife Crisis support groups already exist in most major cities across the country. If a support group does not yet exist in your community, here are several ways to go about forming your own:

- ❖ Post a message on the quarterlifecrisis.com support group forum or on message boards found in similar twentysomething web communities.
- ❖ Advertise in local newspapers or by word of mouth through friends, classmates, and colleagues.
- ❖ Post flyers in coffee shops and college campuses.
- ❖ Organize a group among, for example, your co-workers, classmates, alumni associations, religious groups, or athletic teammates.

Once you have a core group in place, there are several ways to ensure that your meetings will be effective:

- ❖ Meet regularly (i.e., the third Tuesday of every month).
- ❖ Meet in the early evening so that people have time to commute from work.
- ❖ Choose a leader or contact person who is willing to organize meetings and maintain a distribution list.
- ❖ Decide on discussion topics beforehand over email so that participants have time to reflect on their own situations and come up with questions. Examples of possible topics are: dating and relationships, job searching, job satisfaction/fulfillment, finances, current events, networking, or even the latest movies or music.

❖ Encourage members to join special-interest groups together, such as athletic teams, outdoor organizations (hiking, biking), and writing or photography clubs.

There are plenty of other accessible resources that can guide twenty-somethings who are dealing with these quarterlife crisis issues. From books to websites, from family and friends to, yes, therapists, help is out there for you—as long as you are willing to seek it out. You can and will get through your quarterlife crisis. Eventually, with a little bit of patience, determination, and self-acceptance, everybody does.

Topical Index

About the Authors

Alexandra Robbins, author of *Secrets of the Tomb: Skull and Bones, the Ivy League, and the Hidden Paths of Power,* is a contributing writer at *Cosmopolitan* and on the staff of *The New Yorker's* Washington, D.C. Bureau. Formerly a contributing editor at *Mademoiselle*, Robbins has written for several publications, including *The New Yorker, The Atlantic Monthly, The Washington Post, USA Today, Chicago Tribune, Self, PC Magazine, Washington Monthly, Salon, Time Digital, Details, Shape,* and *Journal of Popular Culture.* She graduated from Yale in 1998 and now lives in Washington, D.C.

Abby Wilner graduated from Washington University in St. Louis in 1997 with a degree in psychology and minors in business and music. A series of jobs from arts management to website development, including an ill-fated stint at a dot-com, led her to postsecondary educational research. Abby is the webmaster of *www.quarterlifecrisis.com.* She lives in her native Washington, D.C.

Alexandra and Abby have appeared on *Oprah,* The *Today Show,* The *CBS Early Show,* CNN, MSNBC, NBC News, *The Other Half,* The Oxygen Network, the BBC, and numerous national and local radio programs. The Quarterlife Crisis phenomenon has also been featured in newspapers and magazines across the country, including *The New York Times, USA Today, The Washington Post, Los Angeles Times, Chicago Sun-*

Times, Mademoiselle, New York Daily News, The Philadelphia Inquirer, Detroit Free Press, The Seattle Times, and *National Post (Toronto).*

Quarterlife Crisis was a *New York Times, Wall Street Journal,* and Amazon.com bestseller. A 2001 Amazon.com Editors' Choice, *Quarterlife Crisis* was also nominated for a Books for a Better Life award by the National MS Society.

Both authors continue to be actively involved lecturing to groups about twentysomething issues.